CHICAGO PUBLIC LIBRARY
WOODSON REGIONAL
9525 S HALSTED ST   60628

HQ
734
.C265
199~

WOO~

Chicago Public Library

S0-AOS-220

WOO _____ ...when holidays are hell-- ! : a guid

When Holidays
Are Hell...!

CHICAGO PUBLIC LIBRARY
WOODSON REGIONAL
9525 S HALSTED ST   60628

When Holidays Are Hell...!

A Guide to Surviving Family Gatherings

Mariana Caplan, M.A.

Hohm Press
Prescott, AZ

© Mariana Caplan, 1997
All rights reserved.

No part of this book may be reproduced in any manner
for public or private use without the written permission
of the publisher, except cases of quotes used in reviews.

Layout and Design: Visual Perspectives, Phoenix, AZ
Cover and Bookmark Art: *The Intrigue* by J. Ensor
Koninklijk Museum Voor Schone Kunsten, Antwerpen (België).
Used with permission.

Library of Congress Cataloguing in Publication Data:
Caplan, Mariana, 1969-
   When holidays are hell-- ! : a guide to surviving
   family gathering
/ Mariana Caplan.
   p.   cm.
   Includes bibliographical references (p.).
   ISBN 0-934252-77-7 (alk. paper)
   1. Family. 2. Holiday stress. 3. Adult children--
Family relationships. I. Title.
HQ734.C256 1997   97-2535
646.7'8--dc21   CIP

                 Hohm Press
                 PO Box 2501
               Prescott, AZ 86302
               1-800-381-2700

        http: //www.booknotes.com/hohm/

CHICAGO PUBLIC LIBRARY
WOODSON REGIONAL
9525 S HALSTED ST   60628

Contents

Preface

I admit it, I was a rebellious teenager, and the holidays represented a welcome possibility to wreck havoc on an otherwise monotonous, predictable, and largely superficial (though at times aesthetically pleasing) event.

My initial protest occurred on Thanksgiving Day on my first visit home from college. My date was Spike, an animal-rights activist with cerebral palsy who had a mohawk haircut and an obtrusive cow earring dangling from his left ear. Not only did Spike and I refuse to eat the turkey that was served, as well as the stuffing that had incubated inside of it, but Spike proceeded to expound upon the devastating effects of factory farming on animals to my conservative, middle-class parents, and to detail the dilapidated conditions of the Thanksgiving-turkey concentration camps. As if that weren't enough, later on during the meal, my aunt asked me what I had been studying in college. That was the wrong question! I told her that I had been learning about Native American shamanism and by the way did she know that Thanksgiving was really the celebration of a bunch of Eurocentric white men who conquered, dominated, and subsequently destroyed a group of innocent and earth-loving people who had been occupying the land for hundreds and thousands of years? My appetite to draw attention to the emptiness of our celebration was thoroughly satiated, at the expense of my gracious and well-intentioned family.

Needless to say, things have changed for me since then, but in spite of a one-hundred-eighty-degree turn in attitude, when it comes to the holidays–whether it be Christmas, birthdays, or Mother's Day–and all the hopes, wishes and expectations that accompany these fateful days, it's not easy. Many a parent dreads the moment when their son says, "Mom, please pass the pumpkin pie and by the way I'm gay," or their daughter shows up for Passover with everything but her husband: "Dad, did I remember to mention that Jack and I have decided to get a divorce?" Likewise, many a child lies awake at three A.M. the night before "the big visit" with a pit in his stomach as large as a basketball, wrestling with how to break the big news–whatever the news may be.

You may have picked this book up and be thinking, "I don't need this. I love the holidays. Holidays are fun. What does she mean *survival* guide?" Although you may have three kids you love, an adoring husband, a solid job, parents whom you respect, and a crisp evergreen tree in your cozy living room, you may *still* have some tense moments during the holidays. This is a guide with helpful hints and practical information to ease you over the rough spots.

Personally, I have yet to meet the model, Norman Rockwell family. In most families, there is at least one black sheep; and if it's not you, then it's your lesbian sister or your eccentric uncle. Perhaps you are a single mom, or you spend the holidays with your step-kids, or your father is dying of cancer, or you've just become a vegetarian. Or maybe the whole holiday scene is just so sickeningly perfect and mechanical that you can recite the lines by heart before the guests even arrive. These are the '90s, and the traditional nuclear family is often no longer intact. This is also the era in which many people cannot afford to buy the gifts they wish to give, when the dysfunctional family is the norm, and divorce rates are topping off at fifty percent. Still, families gather together to celebrate, and there *is* a way to make the holiday gathering bearable and even enjoyable.

As a counselor, a clear sign of the approaching holiday season is when my clients come in saying things like, "I know it's wrong to feel this way, but I'm dreading going back East for my parents' fiftieth anniversary party." Or, they suddenly start having ulcers for "no apparent reason," but upon further questioning admit to you that Yom Kippur is rapidly approaching. Holidays often yield depression, loneliness and existential angst. They frequently magnify underlying problems that we have managed to push under the surface in our busy lives. According to the Holmes Rahe Stress Scale, the Christmas season, vacations, and family gatherings provide significant stress factors which affect the body.[1]

The holidays don't have to be hell. There is a lot of generosity, celebration, and genuine, heart-to-heart connecting that is possible during holiday times and family gatherings. The success of your gathering is dependent to a small degree upon what kind of family you are a part of, and a large part on *your attitude,* particularly your sense of priorities and your sense of humor. (Really, there are worse problems in life than your mother predictably boasting about herself as the "Queen of Turkey Stuffing," or your father toasting you and your new husband at your wedding—only calling him by your ex-husband's name!) If the holidays are smooth and easy for you, please do not make them a problem on my account. On the other hand, I encourage you to take advantage of the suggestions offered here that will not only make your holidays and family gatherings more bearable, but may enliven them into true celebrations of sharing and relationship.

---

1 Holmes, T.H., & Rahe, R.H. (1967) The social readjustment rating scale. *Journal of Psychosomatic Research, 11,* 213-218.

Last December I was doing a radio show about the holidays based on my first book, *When Sons and Daughters Choose Alternative Lifestyles* (Prescott, AZ: Hohm Press, 1996). Having given the listeners a brief summary of what I called my "holiday survival guide," a young man called in and asked where he could purchase a copy of this guide. For years I had been writing such a book in my head, and making notes on little reminder cards when I'd visit my folks, thinking that surely *someone else* had written it already. However, after looking in my local public library through 576 entries under the listing "holidays"–entries which described everything from gift ideas, to exotic cookie recipes, to the most obscure holiday celebrations in the farthest reaches of the globe–I discovered that nobody had written a book with the twist that I wanted; a book that empathized with the reader about the difficult situations we sometimes find ourselves in when we go home for the holidays, or when our long grown-up children come home to visit us.

Well, here it is. Take this little book with you in your purse or briefcase, or put the enclosed bookmark in your back pocket before you leave on the trip home, or before the relatives arrive, and start reading it at least once a day. What you will find in these pages is a compendium of useful hints and some necessary comfort.

This book will help you to:

* be hospitable and compassionate with your family,
* learn to laugh at yourself,
* bear the blows gracefully,
* discriminate between myth and reality,
* focus on what's real,
* care for your children's needs,
* and dare to find real meaning amidst holiday havoc.

If your family is together because of a crisis, a death, an accident or the first gathering after any of those, grief may be the prevailing mood. It is true that the pain the family is feeling is deep and needs to be acknowledged, and I have devoted a complete chapter to this important and often overlooked subject.

Let me take this opportunity to wish you all: Feliz Navidad, Merry Christmas, Mazel Tov, Happy Birthday, Happy Hanukkah, Congratulations on your new baby, Thanksgiving greetings, Gung Hey Fat Choy, Happy New Year and Peace to All!

P.S. I'll let you in on a secret. In my family, our dog Buffie, who is now dead, would have eight, wrapped Hanukkah presents—one for each night—on the mantle so that she wouldn't feel left out when everybody else opened their gifts. *Shhh*, don't tell anybody.

1

Why Holidays Can Be Hell...!

Holidays and family gatherings are important in every culture throughout the world. They are a way to mark the passage of time and an opportunity for people to get together, relax and enjoy themselves with the people they care about. Holidays also hold the possibility for spiritual enrichment and reconnection. Yet, before we figure out how to *survive* our family gatherings sanely, it pays to take a good look at what we are trying to survive–what exactly are these events that create such anticipation and such tension in our lives and that consume billions of dollars and hours of time and energy each year *really* about?

Admit it. These high-stress days that have earned a place on the calendar–otherwise known as holidays–are a *big deal.* While family gatherings during the holidays can be times to joyously celebrate and reminisce, it's no small feat to try to fit a whole year's worth of passion and generosity into a couple of days. To attempt to resolve all the family problems on top of this is equivalent to "Mission Impossible."

For the average American, birthdays are a big deal. Anniversaries are a big deal. Easter Sunday in a big deal. Thanksgiving is a big deal. Hanukkah is a big deal. And the biggest deal of all is Christmas.

For some of us, holidays and gatherings are full of questions relative to the family: Whose family to be with? Who will host the event? How will the renegades and misfits get along with everybody else? Who will be upset with whom? There are also the questions of food: How to prepare it? How to tolerate the way others prepare it? How to find something everyone likes to eat? Then there are the dilemmas around gifts–buying them, giving them, receiving and returning them, and the compulsive overspending on credit cards that will take months to pay off.

For many of us, the problem with holidays and family get-togethers is money; for some it is religion or the lack of it; for others, it is interpersonal problems; often it is loneliness and depression. Whatever your "big deal" is, you can be assured that you are not alone, even if you are convinced you are the only one in the world who gets *that* stressed out. Below I have summarized five of the biggest, and some of the most common "big deals" related to holidays and family gatherings in general. Read them over as a way to prepare yourself for the days ahead.

BIG DEAL #1: The "Happy-Together-Family" Gathering is a Myth.

> There we were at the Christmas table—my mother, who was taking tranquilizers to monitor her chronic depression, my distant father, who still doesn't know how to say "I love you" to his kids, my pseudo-Rastafarian little brother, who swore he wasn't stoned that night, my "perfect" sister, who was so uptight that if I lit a match she surely would have exploded, and myself, the political renegade. Is this the kind of family that the classic Christmas tales are written of?

The aura of family harmony and tranquillity so elegantly portrayed by Norman Rockwell does not *exactly* match up with the scene we find in our own living rooms during family get-togethers. Experience tells us that those of us who are gathered around the Thanksgiving dinner table are average neurotic mortals. The bride and groom in the wedding party are human beings, not Cinderella & Co. The couple whose golden anniversary party you are attending have had just as many marital problems as you have. Therefore, according to reason, the holidays are going to be as imperfect as the people who participate in them. Yet, we collectively insist on the childhood myth that simply because it is December 25th, or our daughter's wedding, or because the annual family picnic has appeared on the calendar, suddenly all the problems that were present on the other 364 days of the year will instantly dissipate–that bossy moms will stop bossing, that alcoholic sisters will stop drinking, that rebellious children will cease to turn the holiday upside down.

The "Family Christmas" represents the archetype of the quintessential moment of childhood innocence, and, whether we recognize it consciously or not, many of us will do *almost anything* to try to recreate that moment, even if it never really existed anywhere but in our imaginations. In their innocence, children are able to overlook many subtleties that adults cannot ignore. Consistently failing to acknowledge this, adults idealize the holidays and attempt to reaffirm the "fantasy family" relationship that they wish they had in their childhood.

As children, many adults *did* experience some joyous holidays. Perhaps these only lasted for a couple of years until their parents split up, or for a few precious hours while the presents were being opened and pictures were

being taken. But even if happy holiday memories consti-
tuted only a single scene that fit the advertised ideal, they
made their imprint. Regardless of evidence to the oppo-
site, we still want to think that one or more of these days
is exemplary of the entire year, instead of the exception to
the rule.

Because such a big deal is made of the holidays for
children, our bodies, as adults, will still anticipate eating
special foods, receiving a storehouse of gifts, and being
treated affectionately by all those around us. Like the
grown-up children that we still are, we may feel that special attention is our due, simply because it is the holidays.
Yet expectations are like helium balloons–no matter how
high they rise or how long they fly, eventually they are
destined to fall to the ground.

There is a big legend about holidays in our country that
is handed down from generation to generation–a highly
specific form of cultural programming based upon a
Judeo-Christian upbringing that practically demands that
we look, feel, and act a certain way during the holidays.
The culture (via the media) presents a vision of beatitude,
personal closeness and euphoria so immense that it is vir-
tually impossible for any one family to live up to it. Dr.
Simone Rodin, clinical psychologist at the California
Pacific Medical Center, explains, "There is a much greater
demand to be happy during the holidays [than at any other
time during the year]. It is a pressure that is felt by one

and all to act and feel a certain way that people imagine everybody else is feeling."

The desire to give and receive love and to find meaning in our lives is certainly not a myth. However, most of us do not consciously articulate these desires, and the consumer society takes advantage of this lack of awareness by overtly and subliminally suggesting that this joy can be found in a new sweater, or a cheesecake, or a drunken holiday bash. The media promises that gratification exists within the superficial and material aspect of things, whereas what we really want is something deep and immaterial. We long to feel joy and a sense of belonging, a connection to our families that is outside of conventional materialism.

Any special day that represents this possibility of belongingness becomes a metaphorical carrot that we reach for with all of our might. We cling to the holiday as if it was the answer to our longing, and then, regardless of how it turns out, we pretend it is what we want it to be. So even when the holiday is miserable, we often reaffirm the illusion that everybody has had a splendid time. In other words, some of us muscle up some compassion, or put on a happy smile, and then convince ourselves that all is well. At the end of the day, however, we find that turning to external circumstances to fill an internal void hasn't worked. We either wind up feeling disappointed and ripped off, or we fail to tell ourselves the truth and instead simply comment on how "nice" everything was as we kiss ourselves goodnight.

Family gatherings often present a confusing predicament. Viewed through one lens, you see smiling people and hear clinking glasses atop a background of festive music; from another perspective, you sense people's ulterior motives, feel the pervasive personal insecurity and observe the haze around their sometimes "eggnogged" eyes. You see it, but you don't know what to do about it, and are left with an unsettling question in your mind.

The eventual collapse of the perfect family myth is as inevitable as the realization that Santa is just another guy with a big belly who is getting paid to dress up in red. At some point, you recognize that the holidays probably won't be any different this year than they have been every other year. You know that as soon as the same people get together, the same arguments, tensions and power plays will surface, and you will again be faced with the inevitable recognition that you are with the same family that has had the same problems for the past thirty-seven years.

Most of us sense somewhere within ourselves the gap between how things are "supposed" to be and how they really are. Nonetheless, as we watch the magical day approaching on our calendar (whichever of the magical days it happens to be), or are made aware of it by the imposing cultural indications (Christmas trees, tinsel and lights in every shop window, on every street corner and dotted throughout the neighborhood are hard to miss!), we cannot help but have that small thought in the back of our minds, even if it is not voiced, "Maybe this year it will be different."

The point of all of this is to *know* that you are up against a myth as large as a polar bear at the North Pole, and to *remember* this when you may start to feel like everybody *but* you is having a wonderful time, or when the thought pops into your mind that you should *want* to get drunk and watch the ball drop in Times Square *just because* it is New Year's Eve. When you are able and willing to separate fact from fiction and see things objectively, you'll find greater appreciation for *whatever* kind of holiday you are having!

BIG DEAL #2: The Sacred Is Often Nowhere To Be Found On "Holy-Days."

> *My mother becomes a devout Catholic for ten minutes every Christmas Eve. The rest of the year she is non-practicing. The word "Mass" is a four-letter word to her. Yet, when it comes to the Christmas Eve dinner and a table full of guests, she is suddenly talking about Jesus and the Lord.*

For many of us, the aspect of the "spiritual" during the holidays creates ambivalence and confusion. Often we feel uneasy about the ritualistic and religious elements of the celebration, and confused as to why we are celebrating something that we might not even understand. I was raised in a Jewish family that did not celebrate Christmas, but did a big Hanukkah extravaganza to compensate for the Christmas craze. (Hanukkah, contrary to the popular misconception that it is the Jewish equivalent of Christmas, is actually not one of the holiest days on the Jewish calendar.) Many other Jewish families, however, do exchange gifts with one another and have big meals in their homes on Christmas Day, and I can't blame them. The spiritual aspects aside, Christmas is a massive wave that sweeps over the whole nation. If you're sitting on the shore because its not your turn to swim while everybody else is surfing high, you're probably going to feel left out.

"Christmas in my family was about football," responded one woman when I asked her what the holidays meant to her. "At ten in the morning the TV was on and it was a twelve-hour stretch of turkey sandwiches and Christmas cookies. Thanksgiving was the same–a parade and then football." Leaving the "holy" part of the holiday behind has taken its toll on our culture. The quality of inspiration and renewal that the holidays once offered has now largely been replaced by tension and superficiality. A few years ago I went to a Yom Kippur service at an elegant temple with my Jewish cousins. Although I was moved to find a genuinely holy man chanting the prayers and bringing a little bit of God to the few who were listening, as I stood in the balcony I was again struck, as I had been so many times in childhood, with the emptiness of the show going on beneath me: Women tried to outdo one another with the most expensive hat. Heads bobbed up and down in an effort to stay awake as the rabbi gave his sermon. People constantly glanced at their watches, counting the minutes until they could go home and break their holiday fast.

For some, the point of these holy-days is to convince themselves that they have been absolved of sin and have done their duty in God's eyes by showing up at the temple or church and biding their time for a few hours. Others have a deep connection to their faith yet are not tolerant of their children's right to choose. Many are confused because they feel a lack of holiness in the celebrations of religious holidays and a void of spiritual rituals that foster moral virtues.

If you start to feel like something is missing in terms of religion and the holidays, and are questioning whether or not you even care, *know* that you are not alone. Many of us either consciously struggle with these same issues, or have resigned ourselves to a god-less holiday. It is important to consider these questions and to look for small ways to bring more soul into the holidays. I'll try to inspire you and offer some practical help when we discuss this issue in depth in Chapter Seven: Keeping the Faith.

BIG DEAL #3: The Chances Of Finding (Or Receiving) The Perfect Gift For Any Occasion Are About One In Ten Thousand.

> *I arrived at the ski lodge my family had rented for the holidays, and on my bed was a gift from my mother. It was a four-hundred dollar ski outfit! My mother knows I prefer to ski in my favorite old jacket and sweatshirt, but as a fashion consultant she is compelled to buy her thirty-one-year-old son a designer Obermeyer ski jacket so that she doesn't have to be seen with a child who is out of style.*

It's an old familiar story: The Gift That Wasn't Quite Right. Gifts are like aspirin, they are supposed to make everything *better*. Many of us attempt to fill the gaping hole in ourselves through material possessions, a "high" which lasts only as long as a piece of birthday cake or while the dress is in fashion. Madison Avenue has capitalized on the collective wish in order to increase the consumer economy, and it has worked.

Before the holidays lots of people spend an enormous amount of time and energy roaming the shopping malls or flipping catalog pages in a desperate attempt to demonstrate love to their families. Others use gifts, or the lack of gifts, as a way to prove a point.

> *A friend of mine was having trouble in her marriage but the most revealing sign of their impending separation was that her husband did not get her anything for Christmas. The wound she felt by the timing of his deliberate oversight was enormously painful.*

This whole highly-charged drama–the big deal of "the perfect gift"–can be divided into three parts: buying, giving, and receiving.

- **First is the task of buying.** Trying to find the right gifts, in the right sizes and styles, for the right person, can be *stressful.* There you are, the day after Thanksgiving, pulling your hair out as you sit stuck in your fourth hour of rush-hour traffic. When at last you arrive at the store that promises everything, you spend another half-hour driving around looking for a parking space. By the time you get out of your car, you are already exhausted. Since your parking space is in the far end of the parking lot, you must wade through a quarter mile of mud or slush to reach the front entrance. Then, you weave your way into the store, attempting to dodge overstuffed shopping carts and anxious shoppers, all the while trying to keep track of your kids without having to put them on a leash and without losing your temper. You see the astronomical price tags on gifts you know you can't afford but feel obliged to buy, and your stress peaks during the seemingly endless time you spend standing in check-out lines paying with a piece of plastic that you know is a lie. By the time the smiling Santa Claus winks at you and beckons your kids to sit on his lap, you want to clobber him.

There are numerous options to being overwhelmed by the collective shopping spree. One possibility is to not give gifts, altogether. On rare occasions, this works:

The first couple of years that I didn't buy gifts for my family they were a bit miffed. They could not conceive of that possibility. But they know I care about them, and I do randomly buy them gifts throughout the year when I see something I think they would like. Now it really isn't a problem. Sometimes they give me gifts, sometimes they don't, and it's fine either way.

For others, the choice of refraining from gift buying is not an option:

One Christmas I experimented with not exchanging any gifts because I was having a hard time with the excessive materialism of the holiday, not to mention my finances. I told my family I didn't expect gifts from them but they wouldn't hear of it. To this day it is known in the family folklore as "The Christmas that Jodie didn't give anybody gifts."

Making gifts by hand is, for some people, an enjoyable and stress-relieving alternative. For myself, the nicest gift I received this year was a box of homemade cookies sent by overnight mail from my young cousin on the east coast. Baked goods, knitted slippers, candles rolled from sheets of beeswax, or an embroidered pillowcase may mean a lot more to someone than a designer sweater would.

- **Giving gifts can be a sensitive undertaking.** Do you *have* to give a gift to every one of your third-cousins, your brother-in-law's second wife's children, and all the neighbors? Do you have to give gifts to people whom you don't like as well as those you do? How do you decide what to buy someone you don't know very well, or someone who seems to have everything? And what do you do when you see that someone clearly doesn't like your gift in spite of their polite response? These are questions that each of us as individuals need to answer for ourselves, depending on our family tradition, our personal circumstance and our lifestyle. There are no simple answers or rules to be remembered, but overall I think that the "obligation" of gift giving at certain holiday times has gotten seriously out of control, and that somebody has to stop this snowball before it threatens to create an avalanche. That "someone," however, will need a healthy dose of both courage and self-esteem to stand up to the prevailing cultural mindset, a few ounces of humility so as not to become a righteous crusader, and a pound or two of love and honor for themselves in the process.

One helpful guideline to keep in mind when it comes to giving gifts, is to give something that the receiver might like instead of something you want to give them. The classic example of the husband buying his wife an electric drill for their anniversary is not make-believe. If you really know nothing about your son's third wife, call her up and ask her for a "wish list" instead of buying her something you really want for yourself.

Some people have been known to use gifts as a blatant form of manipulation. Consider this sad example:

The first thing my mother said to me when I walked in the door after I moved to the farm with my kids was, "I'm going to give you a present. I'm going to take you to the mall tomorrow morning and get your hair cut." I was extremely insulted and hurt.

Whatever you decide to give, make it personal. A card with a simple handwritten message on it may mean a lot more to your family members than one that simply has your name typeset across the bottom.

You are almost always safe giving the gift of edibles. (Who can refuse chocolates, or a gift certificate to a good restaurant in their town?) Tickets to *The Nutcracker* or a special performance of Handel's *Messiah* can also be a way to bring a personal touch to holiday gift giving.

• **Receiving gifts can be an uplifting and joyful celebration, or it can be an unpleasant interchange.** The former is the result of having an "attitude of gratitude" and few expectations, and the latter, a consequence of adherence to the equation "gifts = love." Some of us are embarrassed to receive gifts and do not know how to respond given the pressure we feel to react appropriately.

My brother and sister-in-law have no idea who I am. A year ago they gave me a gift set of gourmet coffees. Coffee is not in my world—I have never drank it my whole adult life. In spite of my best efforts, my face must have gone funny because they looked at me and said, "Don't you drink coffee?" I lied, "Of course, once in awhile I drink it, and it will be great for entertaining."

If you have a lot invested in getting a certain gift from a particular person, or if you measure someone's affection for you by the gift he or she gives you, you are setting yourself up for disappointment. On the other hand, if you can receive a gift as a gesture of another person's regard and affection for you, even if they do give you a monogrammed handkerchief for the third year in a row, you will treasure the present, just the same.

One man I spoke with has managed to reconcile the inevitable disenchantment that so many face when they don't get the right gift. He told me, "I always get what I want because I never expect *anything*, so whatever I get is fine." If you are able to have his perspective, you too will always be happy.

Often people try to wrap their emptiness up in pretty paper and put a ribbon around it, hoping that by disguising their pain it will go away. That strategy rarely works. Instead, the holidays can be a time to focus on authentic relationship, the good company of others and the real things we give each other. Then, the receiving of gifts is a symbol of care and attention, no matter what form the gift is in.

BIG DEAL #4: Some Of Us Treat Our Dogs Better Than We Treat Our Family; And Sometimes The Family Commands Less Respect Than Our Pets.

Can you imagine spending time at the home of your dearest and most respected friend and leaving your bed unmade? Or refusing to take out the garbage because it wasn't your turn? Or lounging in front of the television set for hours, gradually clearing out the 'fridge of goodies while your host cooked and cleaned for you, working overtime to keep the electricity bill paid? Probably not! Yet this is precisely how many thirty-, forty-, and fifty-year-old "kids" treat their families when they go home for the holidays. These same people could not imagine treating their pets with such little respect and consideration.

Our daughter came off the airplane in a pair of oversized overalls and a ripped shirt. In those days people really dressed up when they traveled. We had spent so much money on her "going away to college" clothes that we were

*very embarrassed to see her come off the plane
dressed in her "early Salvation Army" look.*

Family is perhaps the greatest challenge that human beings face. On one hand, even if you only see them once every three years, you feel an inexplicable bond and loyalty to these people with whom you share similar genes. On the other hand, if you weren't related you might have nothing in common with your family members and might never choose to even speak with these people if you happened to sit next to one of them on a park bench. More so today than ever, as a result of the skyrocketing presence of divorce, neglect, and all forms of abuse, many people are filled with tremendously conflicting emotions when it comes to family. There is a lot of external pressure during holiday times which can heighten and magnify any existing difficulties in the family–a tension which can be more easily glossed over if you live two thousand miles away, or if you ordinarily have no time in your life to consider such problems. There is an expectation that everybody should get along beautifully simply because it is your brother's wedding or Mother's Day.

Some of us seem to think that just because this woman called "Mother" wiped our nose for the first three years of our life that we have permission to insist that she do the same throughout our adulthood. Just because we have a similar DNA as our brothers and sisters, we assume that this is an excuse to treat them worse than we treat our friends.

The flip side of this equation is that many families command less respect than our dogs do. When we get home from work, our pets will often jump into our laps, lick our toes, or anxiously follow us around the house (even if it *is* just food that they want). When we show up at the old homestead for a family reunion, however, it is entirely possible that within the first five minutes our mother will say something off-handedly insulting, like, "I guess you've learned how to cook well–you're so ... *big.*" Or our son may comment, "You've brought so much luggage you'd think you were trying to move in."

Sometimes we treat our families worse than we do our pets because our families aren't our intimates anymore. We have lost the model of the close-knit extended family, and therefore when families get together, all the focus is on food and gifts, as these are the only semi-reliable staples amidst the spoken and unspoken turmoil. But when the reliable elements are gone–you've opened all the gifts or you've eaten so much that you can't even stand the thought of one more bite–you're once again left with the reality of your imperfect family.

When there is nothing solid to hold them together, families resort to guilt to try to stay connected. I had a client who honestly believed that if he did not go back to his folks' house to participate in the holidays, this meant that he was an uncaring and mean-spirited son. It didn't help that his mother had called him up two weeks before Christmas and whined to him that she knew he wasn't coming home because, "I had been such a bad mother," and that it was unfortunate that he could not be more forgiving. I spoke with one mother who decided against a trip to Hawaii over the holidays because she was concerned that her "kids"–ages thirty-seven and thirty-nine–wouldn't be able to make Christmas dinner properly if left to their own resources, and she felt responsible for it.

It is not uncommon for a grandparent to say things like, "I want to be able to dance at your wedding, so you had better hurry up and get married 'cause I won't be able to dance too much longer." Or, "You've always been my favorite grandchild, other than the fact that you're not married." If we cannot sustain the family bond through intimacy and organic affection, many will grasp at straws and attempt to use guilt to coerce the rest of the family into a feeling of pseudo-completeness. It's kind of like feeding your poodle so he will follow you around. You soon convince yourself that he really *loves* you.

Holidays in my family seem to be little more than a time to dredge up old expectations and failures ... about how I'm forty years old and still not married, or about how the Jews have

*fought for 40,000 years for their heritage and
I'm going to destroy it in a single generation.*

Family skeletons, whose permanent residency is in the
closet, tend to creep out over holidays, lured by the irre-
sistible attraction of turkey dinners and anniversary
cakes. They also creep out from behind the doors, from
under the rug, from backyard treehouses .... Every family
has got their secrets, often lots of them, and these tend to
reveal themselves at the most inauspicious moments,
striking anxiety and even terror into our hearts.
Unfortunately, some family members use these secrets as
ammunition for war–trying to hurt back those who have
victimized them.

Families *are* a big deal, and learning how to treat your
closest kin as well as you treat your dog (even when Fido
rolls around in the mud and shakes out all over you) is a
worthwhile endeavor. It takes hard work, attention and
commitment to be kind and generous with our relatives. It
takes maturity and sensitivity to honor and respect the
needs of others, especially if they are not honoring or
respecting ours. It takes guts to draw realistic and caring
boundaries to preserve our own well-being and that of our
children. But the efforts are certainly worthwhile.

BIG DEAL # 5: The Pressure Is Great To Go Home.

"You mean I don't *have* to go home for the holidays?!" exclaimed one client, when I made that suggestion because of her present emotional state. The internal pressure to go home that this woman felt was so strong that she did not even realize she had a choice in the matter. Countless other adults feel the same way, as I've learned over the years.

If it works to go home, by all means go, but sometimes you're better off not going. Although this may not be received graciously by your relations, it's no reason to sulk around feeling sorry for either yourself or your family. Lots of mature people who love their families very much still decide to skip the trip, without having to lie or justify themselves.

If you're standing at the crossroads, wary of going home for the holidays, you have a couple of choices. Consider first of all that it's all right to skip a wedding, a funeral or a holiday *just because* you don't *feel* like going. It doesn't mean you don't love your family. You just might not want to travel, pure and simple. It's okay to break convention even if there are no big emotional reasons for doing so.

If you *must* have a justifiable excuse for staying home from a family gathering, here are eight good reasons not to go:

1.) If you have emotionally or physically abusive parents or children, or if there are individuals or other influences in the environment that present a physical or emotional threat to your children.

If you're twenty-one years old, and your mother still threatens to lock you out of the house if you're not home by midnight; if your husband and father get into a slugging match every Fourth of July; or if your kids are whining three weeks in advance about having to go to Grandma's for Easter because she spanks them when they misbehave, *reconsider your plans.*

When there has been abuse in a family, maintaining boundaries around privacy or personal space may still be a big issue. When someone is healing from abuse and suddenly returns home, they are unlikely to be received with open arms within an abusive family structure.

There is value in maintaining tradition and doing things for no other reason than to please those you love, but it is also important to recognize an abusive environment for what it is, and to make a definitive choice not to place yourself and/or your children in a situation where they may be mistreated.

2.) If you have spent six months and/or a thousand dollars in therapy considering how to "break the news" to your family that you won't be there.

If you always get a fever three days before Christmas, or if the atmosphere in your whole house turns into an emotional mayhem because you're so stressed out about the family visit, reconsider the whole idea of participating in the family gathering. The holidays are not supposed to be a dreaded event. If things are so terrible that your decision not to go is itself a family crisis, you are well advised to break this insane cycle and consciously decide to spend a quiet holiday with friends, or with your partner and children.

3.) If you or your chosen lifestyle is the main course of the meal.
If the fact that you are a white woman with a black child is the dominant discussion over dinner, or if your rebellious kids refuse to accept your renewed interest in Orthodox Judaism, spend the holidays with someone who appreciates you more. If your parents or children insist that everything was going smoothly until *you* walked in the door, save everybody the trouble. If they can't blame their problems on you, you may actually be doing your family a favor.

4.) If you are participating in the family gathering to be a martyr and/or to save the family.
If you think that *your* presence at the family reunion is going to keep your parents from splitting up, your child from drinking, or that in one visit you can psychoanalyze

and heal forty years of family problems, you're going for the wrong reasons. It is not possible to effect a change in the family structure overnight.

5.) If you can't leave your past behind to enjoy the present.
If you can't lay aside your past resentments for the duration of two days, and the whole visit is a rehashing of problems that nobody but you wants to discuss, don't bother going home.

6.) If your motivation for going stems purely out of guilt.
Guilt is a useless, though pervasive, emotion in the Judeo-Christian culture. Going home for the holidays because you don't want to face the guilt you will feel if you don't go is not a good enough reason. You will wind up feeling resentful at your hosts at the least sign of not being appreciated. Discover the roots of your guilt and deal with those instead of acting for false purposes.

7.) If you can't afford it.
If your relatives are insisting you come, but you can't afford it and they don't offer to help, it is fine to decline. Be reasonable and use your common sense.

8.) If you're going to have to spend more than three days recovering from the visit.

If the holidays are so exhausting and draining that you end up in bed with an emotional hangover for the next week, it's probably costing you more than it's worth to go.

Be gracious and tactful when you tell your parents or your children that you're not coming, or not hosting, this year. In many families, if you try to explain that you're not going home because your self-esteem is too low, or that the family neurosis is going to set you back years in therapy, they will misunderstand and probably feel hurt and upset. It is fine to tell them that you can't take off of work, that you have other plans, or that you can't afford it. Perhaps you can make an alternative date with them at a less stressful time, but if you do, be sure to follow through with it.

There are other ways to share yourself with your family during holiday times without actually going home. One client who decided not to visit his elderly mother sent her a video he made of his home, friends, and local tourist sights that he thought would be interesting to her. It was a loving gesture that made her feel cared for during the holiday season. Another woman, who was having a difficult time in her therapy, chose not go to her cousin's wedding, but contributed by generously helping the family to get plane tickets for the distant relatives. On the practical side, a conference-call home to wish everyone well brings your best regards to family members in the midst of their party. You can drop in for three minutes and everybody's happy. You will communicate that your choice to stay home is not a withdrawal of your love for your family by the mood in which you hold your contact with them.

The holidays are a big deal. The point is not to get involved in a big-deal depression, but to recognize the big deals for what they are and enjoy the holidays free from their domination.

REMEMBER:

BIG DEAL #1: The "Happy-Together-Family" gathering is a myth.

We have idealized the holidays to confirm the fantasy family relationship we *wish* we had in childhood. Be clear about separating fact from fiction.

BIG DEAL #2: The sacred is often nowhere to be found on "holy-days."

Something may be missing during the holidays and it often is the spiritual aspect of the celebration. Look for small ways to bring more soul into your family gathering.

BIG DEAL #3: Your chances of finding (or receiving) the perfect gift are about one in ten-thousand.

Buying gifts, giving gifts and receiving gifts can be joyful or unpleasant. Remember to focus on authentic relationships and the good company of relatives and friends during the holidays rather than bemoaning the wrong size shirt or the Day-Glo–green hat.

BIG DEAL #4: Some of us treat our dogs better than we treat our family; and sometimes the family commands less respect than our pets.

Family gatherings unleash tremendous stress and are often challenging opportunities to practice understanding, patience and kindness.

BIG DEAL #5: The pressure is great to go home.

If you don't want to spend the holidays with your family, don't go home; but if you decide to go, be friendly, generous and remind yourself to be a happy guest.

2

Family Psychology In Seven Easy Lessons

Now that you've gotten an overview of why the holidays and family gatherings can be such a "big deal" in our culture, I will give you a close-up look into the inner workings of the family. A cursory understanding of family psychology, which I will present to you in seven easy lessons, will help you understand the dynamics at play when families gather, so that if or when things fall apart you don't end up taking it all personally.

When many of us hear the word "psychology" we immediately imagine ourselves lying on a couch, being scrutinized. However, psychology doesn't have to be that way. Psychology is just a way of understanding why we act the way we act and do the things we do, so that if we want to make a change in our lives, we have the tools with which to do so.

LESSON NUMBER ONE:
The Family Psychology Is Bigger Than You Are.
Technical Term: Psychological Genealogy

> *When I first began to study psychology, I couldn't believe all the implications of my dreams. I was amazed at how my father's stories about the war showed up in my dreams—I was actually fighting a war, with a loaded gun in my hand. However, when I began to understand something deeper about family psychology, I began to see how strongly bonded family members are, and that my dreams might be reflecting aspects of his life as well as my own.*

The individual, family, and collective psychologies that you are a part of are *bigger than you.* You are subject to influences within yourself that you have little or no control of as part of a bigger whole. There is a "family mind" doing much of the thinking for your entire household, and you are simply one small segment of this mind. There is a cultural mentality about the holidays in your environment which is so large that your personal opinions about the holidays may stand little chance against it.

Children tend to "become" their parents. That "independent," "unique" "individual" that you are staring at in the mirror is little more (and little less) than the sum total of generation upon generation of your forefathers and foremothers mixing and matching and learning and evolving, plus a touch of your very own personal spirit. The special little family you call your own is the child of your ancestors' families. Just as an individual's genetic make-up is the result of tens of thousands of years of mating, so too is our psychological make-up a combination of all the neuroses, aberrations, and adaptations of our particular lineage up until the time of our birth.

Use this knowledge not as an excuse to stay under the covers while the holidays pass, but to take the burden of the "perfect family" celebration off your own shoulders. Give yourself and others in your family a little breathing space around the usual Christmas crises; forgive the family foibles that are an inevitable part of the holiday heirloom.

LESSON NUMBER TWO:
A Family Gathering Produces A Trance State.
Technical Term: Hypnosis

> *My girlfriend never watches TV, and is generally a gregarious and happy person. Needless to say, I was more than surprised when we went to visit her family for Passover one spring and within the first hour she was flopped down in front of the television like a couch potato. She*

rarely moved from that spot for the next seven days.

There is a kind of hypnotic induction that occurs when we gather for a family event–a family trance in which you suddenly become the person you were when you were twelve years old; or you regress to treating your kids like they were twelve. It is one of those mysteries of the world–suddenly you are a forty-five-year-old teenager too nervous to ask your mother if you can borrow her car. Or you may find yourself speaking to your fifty-two-year-old daughter as though she were still a teenager.

The hypnotist is not one person per se, but the momentum gained from the re-enactment of the same ritual time and time again. Everybody knows how the holiday or family event is supposed to go, and so we often flip onto automatic pilot. That hypnotic state will then effortlessly carry us along.

Another scenario: hundreds of memories come rushing back to your mind the minute you park the car in the cul-de-sac where you spent ten carefree years playing flashlight tag and kickball, or the instant you walk into the house that is permeated with that smell you could never forget, or when you notice that half the photographs on the wall of the den are of you at age five. When your father starts calling you "Little Susie," and your Mom bakes a batch of your favorite cookies, something gets a little blurry and you mysteriously find yourself back in the familiar family trance.

Or perhaps your married daughter opens the door with her old key, calls out to you, "Mom, I'm home," and suddenly you find yourself thinking about the old days, feeling happily nostalgic or upset.

As for myself, I find this phenomenon recurring whenever I visit my family's country home. I get trapped into an eleven-year-old mentality. Instead of being a confident and contented professional, fifty percent of the time I am mousy quiet and distant, with a chip on my shoulder and an attitude problem. Fortunately, the other half of the time I am able to splash some cold water on my face and wake up enough to take advantage of my short visit, engaging my relatives in pleasant conversation and being myself as an adult.

Aside from the lack of awareness that defines this hypnotic state, the real problem is that some of us say and do very inconsiderate things when in such a trance. For example, if your father is buzzed out on his second six-pack and sitting in front of the football game, he may start ordering you around: "Go to the kitchen and get me some chips." When your son is in a trance he may start teasing your daughter, calling her names she hasn't heard for twenty years. When *you* are in a trance you may start expecting your mother to do the dishes for you even though you've been doing them yourself for the past thirty years, or you may start nagging your kids to finish everything on their plates.

The best thing you can do when you find yourself floating in the family trance is to try to stay as awake as possible—and that's not easy when the slumber of ignorance is seducing you into bed with it. It's like driving at two A.M. in a car full of sleeping people. You just want to snooze right along with them. Nonetheless, despite your weariness, it is your job to stay awake if you wish to stay alive.

You can help break out of a trance at family gatherings by:

- dragging yourself out to take a brisk walk in the middle of an absurd family squabble,
- choosing to eat healthily the day after Christmas when you wake up with a hangover, instead of temporarily resolving the problem with one more beer or five cups of coffee,
- calling up some friends and connecting with someone outside of the family for a reality check,
- taking a cold shower,
- putting on some unusual music and dancing around your room—whatever it takes to remind you that you are distinct from your environment and to shake off the family sleep.

LESSON NUMBER THREE:
Even Fifty-Year-Old "Kids" Want Their Parents' Approval.
Technical Term: Mirroring

> "My twenty-one-year-old daughter Julie had told us that her boyfriend had longish hair," began one father, a retired factory worker, "but when I happened to look out the window on the day before Christmas and saw this seedy looking, six-foot-three-inched guy with flaming red hair down his back and an electric guitar draped over his shoulder, it suddenly hit me that this was the one. I was only half joking when I said to Julie, 'Couldn't he have waited to come until after dark so the neighbors wouldn't see him?' "

Julie wasn't completely honest with her parents about her boyfriend because she feared losing their approval–and with good reason! Everyone wants acknowledgment and approval no matter how old they are. Even if your nineteen-year-old son comes home from college with his ear pierced, he is still craving your acknowledgment. It is not uncommon for an adult woman to start feeling uncomfortable when her mother doesn't comment on how thin she looks within the first five minutes after she's stepped off the plane.

All of us care what others think about us, even those of us who proudly boast we don't. The psychological principle of mirroring states that in childhood we come to know ourselves by how our environment responds to us. A child's essence, creativity, and essential goodness long to emerge, and these qualities are dependent upon whether his parents reflect these back to him from an early age. Conversely, a lack of mirroring often results in a child who may be hostile and emotionally unstable because she does not trust her world. Therefore, if we did not get the validation that we needed in childhood (and many parents in the past several generations have not known how to do this successfully), we will continue to seek confirmation and acknowledgment as adults.

A further complication in the child's need for mirroring is that our parents have become *internalized* within us, meaning that because of the immense influence they had on our psychological development, we have taken them into ourselves and they are alive inside our own minds. Therefore, it's not only our parents "in the flesh" that we are seeking acknowledgment and validation from, but also the parental voices within ourselves that we are trying to answer to. Even if our actual parents died years ago, we are still trying to please and appease them in this way.

Although everyone *wants* acceptance and approval, it is possible to grow yourself up so that you don't *need* it.

Just because you're thirty years old does not mean you are grown up. True adulthood is much more than biological maturity. It is the ability to make good choices, access common sense, and be objective, especially during times of emotional or physical stress. You wean yourself from the obsessive drive for acknowledgment by seeing the backbends and somersaults you constantly do for it, and you decide that such back strain just isn't worth it.

LESSON NUMBER FOUR:
If We Imagine That Our Brother Is Out To Get Us, That's How We'll Relate To Him As He Walks In The Door.
Technical Term: Projection

> *Just because my father was disapproving about anything I did, I assumed my father-in-law would feel the same way, and wanted to jump down his throat in self-defense when he even looked my way, even if it was just to make a friendly comment. It took me years to understand that it was my father who disapproved of me, not every man in the world!*

This is how projection works. For me, the moment I finally "got" the meaning of projection was the highlight of my academic career as a graduate psychology student. I was stunned. My professor had just explained that when you go to the cinema, you experience the movie as being on the screen in front of you, although it is actually inside the projector behind you. He explained that, similarly, projections are crystallized thoughts and ideas about someone or something that exists *in your own mind* (i.e., the projector), that you subsequently place onto someone or something outside of yourself (i.e., the screen), and thereby proceed to live as if it was occurring in the exterior world.

The consequence of projection is that you succeed in creating the subjective reality that you imagine. You alone make your sweetest dreams come true, as well as your most terrifying nightmares. If you believe that your cousin hates you, the minute he walks in the church for the wedding you start relating to him defensively. You *will* find evidence of your belief in everything that he does, everything that he says, every one of his gestures and expressions, even though he's as harmless as an angel. If you are convinced that your children have abandoned you because they've decided not to come home for the family reunion on the 4th of July, you will use this fact to confirm your belief, and carry a grudge for years.

When you can allow others to be even a shade different from how you expect them to be, you have begun to mature. For example, if you are talking to your once-delinquent nephew whom you haven't seen for ten years, perhaps you can remind yourself that there are all kinds of unconscious ways you are relating to him based upon your past ideas about who he was, leaving no room for new impressions. When you give someone the benefit of the doubt in your mind, you'll not only find more patience inside yourself but will be surprised to find that they may not be exactly as you had imagined them to be.

Once we recognize that we participate in creating the images that our families have *about us*, we can take responsibility for those images. Then there is a possibility for change. When we cease to project onto others, others cease to reflect these projections back to us. If somebody refuses to play, the game is off.

LESSON NUMBER FIVE:
We All Conspire To Do Everything We Can To Keep Everyone In Their Traditional Family Role.
Technical Term: Homeostasis

> *"Mine is a family of Jews," shared one mother. "We all came over on the boat to Ellis Island and it is our duty to maintain the customs and rituals of Judaism. So when my son brought home his Mormon girlfriend from college, I went into shock. What could I say? I loved my*

> *son but his behavior was entirely unacceptable*
> *within our family tradition.*

The family can be likened to an ecosystem. Each element of the system affects and is affected by all the others. What would a rainforest do without rain? This is how the family system is altered when instead of getting married, having babies, and moving onto the same block as all your cousins and grandparents, you take off to the other side of the country and start making your living as an urban newspaper reporter, writing poetry at night. It doesn't fit. The same thing happens when your kids offer to prepare Thanksgiving dinner at *your* Italian-Catholic household and they place a Chinese feast on your table instead. It throws off the balance by breaking with custom.

The family system needs stability and equilibrium to sustain itself, and will try to maintain the balance that was set up in the early years of its creation. If a foreign element is introduced into the system, the family will either attempt to expel it (Mother quickly calls a local restaurant and orders in a traditional Thanksgiving dinner and puts the Chinese food in the 'fridge), or to ignore the intrusion and quietly attempt to absorb it (the whole family sits silently around the table without mentioning that their forks have been replaced with chopsticks).

– Family Psychology In Seven Easy Lessons –

I have a friend who has a reputation in his family for being cold-hearted because he was a loner in childhood. As an adult, he is actually one of the most loving people I know, but his family still overlooks most signs to the contrary and maintains his role (in their own minds) for him by forever repeating the stories of how withdrawn he is. He just goes along his merry way, being kind and considerate, and lets them continue to think he is cold-hearted, without judging them. For others stuck in a family role, however, the consequences are not so easily dismissed. Admittedly, it's tough to break out of being labeled the family "ne'er do well," for instance. Many people make the mistake of believing that a label once applied has to last forever; and the reinforcement which the family pours on doesn't help support a breakthrough.

For better or worse, you *do* have a place in your family system–and it greatly helps if you recognize what it is, i.e., who you are to them, so that this "role" doesn't define and limit who you are to *you*. You are then left with a number of choices. You can aggressively try to create a revolution in the family system, which will undoubtedly mean some upset; or you can recognize that others' opinions of you are really not your business, and quietly go about your life among the relatives, watching for the subtle traps that will reinforce the old play, and sidestepping them whenever possible. You can be *in* the family but not embroiled in the family dynamic, simply by maintaining an attitude of relaxed detachment–one small step back from the fray.

LESSON NUMBER SIX:
We Can Stuff The Turkey, But Stuffing The Family Pain Will Leave Us With Emotional Indigestion. Technical Term: Denial

Denial is mind-boggling. The Loch Ness monster can be sitting at the head of your dining room table, but if you don't want to see ol' Nessie, you won't notice her. We will go to enormous lengths in order to avoid the pain of seeing or feeling something we don't want to know about–and in all families, every member has "stuff" about themselves and the others that they would rather not be faced with. Denial is the amazing ability of the human mind, as well as the family mind, to convince itself that reality is other than it actually is.

Human beings are imperfect–it's just the way things are. Sisters are sometimes jealous of each other. Brothers fight. Parents are often neglectful (or worse) towards their kids. Sons and daughters can be thoughtless towards Mom and Dad. If we are unable to face the abundant evidence of human imperfection, we will sink into deeper and deeper denial, insisting on the childhood myth that we have a "perfect family."

– Family Psychology In Seven Easy Lessons –

We live in a crazy world and are the products of all of those who came before us. What is *is*. We can't change the past. Until we accept it for what it is, there is pain. When we admit to the fact that there are some problems in the family, we cease having to run around like chickens with our heads cut off trying to keep ourselves so busy that we have no time to notice; or we cease having to keep our heads in the sand like ostriches, pretending everything is fine.

Admitting that there *are* problems does not mean we have to solve them, or draw everyone in the family into the drama of them. Admitting our family's (and our own) imperfections can be a very quiet and personal thing. The important part is not to stuff them down, feigning ignorance. Only by first *admitting what is* can we ever make the next step–*accepting what is*. And that's what we call *compassion*.

LESSON NUMBER SEVEN:
Nothing Is Going To Change Until *We* Change (And Even Then, *They* Will Probably Stay The Same). Technical Term: Mechanicality

The family gathering is pre-recorded:

I can accurately predict that I'll have a fight with my mother while getting the meal ready. I will probably storm out. Some father or uncle or brother will come back to get me. I'll be in a bad mood for the first five minutes until I'm joked out of it, and then we'll all have a good time.

Families are predictable. Human beings ordinarily operate in a mechanical, predetermined fashion. This year at the family picnic, for instance, you can expect that Aunt Elsie will bring the same fruit salad with marshmallows, even if nobody's eaten it for the past five years. When people get drunk on New Year's Eve, we know what happens. We probably know that ten minutes after a political discussion begins in our family that there will be a fight, or that if Liza forgets to take her Valium before the Bar Mitzvah party that everybody is going to pay for it. Oftentimes we can even predict what somebody will say before they say it.

- 46 -

Don't expect things to be different–ever. Occasionally they will change, but it is probably not the result of your doing. If you want anything to change, *you* need to be the one who is different. Adopt a new attitude or change a few simple habits. If you can foster an alternative perspective, a whole new world opens up. For instance:

• **Redefine "Reality":** Decide that the reason your father incessantly criticizes you is because that's the only way he knows how to express his love. When he starts in on you, you can say to yourself, "Thanks for caring for me, Dad."

• **Shut Up and Listen:** Realize that when your daughter stomps out of the house after an argument that she is trying to get your attention, and wants to feel your love; let her know that you care about her and will listen to her side of the story.

• **Take a Break:** If you get worked up into an uncontainable fury over the trite conversation during the Sabbath dinner, find a kid at the table who can't sit through the adult talk and invite them to go outside to play with you.

• **Give In, with Love:** If your mother asks you when you'd like to come over to celebrate Christmas and exchange gifts and what you'd like to have for dinner, you can simply and graciously say that it is up to her–that you will be happy to come whenever she'd like, and will enjoy whatever she'd like to serve. Her gratitude for that small shift may change everything. One friend reported that, "It was both wonderful and painful for me to realize how easy it would have been to have practiced that little bit of kindness, generosity and compassion toward my parents for the last twenty years."

•••

Congratulations! In seven short lessons you've completed your first course in family-holiday psychology. Despite your new knowledge, however, recognize that the most critical information is easier to study than to put into action. Here are some quick reminders for you to refer to when you're beginning to be drawn into the family maelstrom.

REMEMBER:

LESSON NUMBER ONE: The Family Psychology Is Bigger Than You Are.
All of us are subject to influences over which we have little or no control. Learn to recognize some of these influences in your family. Relax and forgive yourself and others.

LESSON NUMBER TWO: The Family Gathering Produces A Trance State.

Beware of hypnosis. Try to maintain an alert state of consciousness. Remember, it is important to stay awake if you wish to stay sane during the family gathering.

LESSON NUMBER THREE: Even Fifty-Year-Old Kids Want Their Parents' Approval.

Although everyone wants acknowledgment and love, it is possible to not *need* it. If we can separate childhood from adulthood, we can use our common sense and learn to view situations objectively.

LESSON NUMBER FOUR: If We Imagine That Our Brother Is Out To Get Us, That's How We'll Relate To Him As He Walks In The Door.

We make our sweetest dreams or our darkest nightmares come true. Once we recognize that we participate in creating the images our families have about us and one another, there is a possibility for change.

LESSON NUMBER FIVE: We All Conspire To Do Everything We Can To Keep Everyone In Their Traditional Family Role.

The family operates as a system which needs stability and equilibrium to sustain itself. We each have a place in our family, and our interdependence with each other is undeniable.

LESSON NUMBER SIX: We Can Stuff The Turkey, But Stuffing The Family Pain Will Leave Us With Emotional Indigestion.

Recognize that human beings are imperfect. Accept the past for what is was and accept the present for what it is. Pretending that something isn't happening or didn't happen doesn't support optimal digestion.

LESSON NUMBER SEVEN: Nothing Is Going To Change Until *We* Change (And Even Then, *They* Will Probably Stay The Same).

Don't *expect* things to be different–ever. If you want anything to change, you need to take steps in that direction and be the one who is willing to act differently.

3

Surviving Family Gatherings, *or* Staying Healthy, Healthy And Wise

Even for a person in the peak of good health, the holidays and other family gatherings can be a challenge. The routine stress associated with gift giving, cooking, traveling and overeating takes a toll on our bodies. The many New Year's resolutions we make, and vows we take after family gatherings (99 percent of which are subsequently broken within 1.5 days) are a testimony to the war we wage against our bodies and health during the holiday time.

Addictions run rampant during the holidays, and almost everybody is addicted to something: the spirits in the eggnog, the sugar in the birthday cake, the anaesthetic effect of television or the promises of happiness in shopping. Not only are there *more* addictions available during the holidays, but when the tension is high, as happens at family gatherings, we are more likely to fall into health-negative patterns as a means of soothing ourselves. The holiday or "party" mentality tells us that *more is better*, and that lie gives us permission to overindulge and throw common sense in the trash.

If dessert is usually accompanied by a discussion of Aunt Mary's aches and pains or little Bobby's cute remarks, you may overeat out of sheer boredom (or frustration). If you're a recovering alcoholic but your family won't serve non-alcoholic drinks because the word "sober" isn't in their vocabulary, you may be seriously challenged to maintain your health and sobriety.

Deborah Auletta, nursing supervisor at a hospital in northern Arizona, reported that the emergency room is packed on holidays, with additional staff on call anticipating the rush. "The season (not just Christmas but all major holidays) is stressful, and as a result, the emergency room is very busy. We see many more cardiac problems. The whole mood of the holidays is hard on a person's body—the stress, the anticipation, the shopping, and especially the food. People get food stuck in the esophagus because they are eating so fast. Gall bladder attacks are also common because of all the rich foods that people eat during the holidays."

As I see it, the major holiday health concerns can be grouped into the following four categories: Alcoholism, Dietary Differences, Overeating, and Physical and/or Emotional Dis-Ease.

ALCOHOLISM

While the subject of alcoholism is far too extensive to adequately address here, a few brief reminders are offered to those who are struggling with either their own or a family member's alcohol addictions.

Throughout the nation, the holidays are a kind of "alcoholism on cue," as the following testimony will verify:

> *The holiday tradition among my friends was mimosas at 10 a.m., football and Bloody Mary's at noon, eggnog while we prepared the feast, aperitifs before dinner, wine with the meal, and beer and videos in the evening. Half the pain of being in recovery was the desire to drink the Bloody Mary's, and half was what it was like to be sober in a group of people who were not. I was suddenly looking at the world through a different lens.*

Many of my clients could not imagine what a non-alcoholic holiday would look like: "How do you dance when you're not drunk?" they'd ask. Or, "What is St. Patrick's Day without beer?" (What is it *with* beer?) For alcoholics who are abstaining, a New Year's Eve's bash can be a disaster.

Whether you have a sober household and your kids don't want to come home because you don't serve beer with the football game, or if your parents don't take your recovery seriously and insist on offering you wine with dinner, your relationship to alcohol–whatever it is–will probably be confronted during holidays and other family gatherings.

Some Sound Advice For A Sober Holiday:

- *If you're a person who has a vow not to drink, and your hosts keep insisting, graciously say, "No, thank you,"* rather than trying to expound upon the evils of alcohol to them.

- *If you're in AA* (Alcoholics Anonymous), or even if you aren't but you want some help staying sober, *go to meetings over the holidays.* No matter where you live or your relatives live, you can find an AA chapter there. If you are troubled by a family member's alcoholism, you may find AlAnon meetings (a group for families of alcoholics) and CODA (Codependents Anonymous) helpful as additional support.

- *Bring a friend along to your family party–a friend who supports your commitment to sobriety.* Simply having somebody else present who is behind your choice not to drink can be a tremendous source of strength.

- *Bring your own drinks.* If you think that gin will be the only clear liquid at the gathering, bring along a selection of non-alcoholic drinks or fancy bottled water.

- *If it is an office party that is threatening your sobriety, stop in for fifteen minutes* and pay your respects, then slip out the back door before you're tempted to indulge. Most of the party may be so tipsy and so busy socializing that they will never notice that you didn't stay very long.

- *If your hosts are so threatened by your choice to stay sober that they will do everything but pour it down your throat, don't visit,* yet don't make them feel badly about it. Tell them, "I know you all love me, but the temptation to drink is just too much for me to deal with right now."

- *Don't be a righteous recovering alcoholic.* It puts a damper on the holiday. If you are judging others for their drinking, or feeling superior to them because of your commitment to sobriety, they will feel uncomfortable.

DIETARY DIFFERENCES

This is the age of diverse dietary plans. There are twelve million vegetarians in the United States,[2] and there are those who keep kosher and those who eat fat free, salt free, cholesterol free, sugar free, and caffeine free. Some people are on diets for reasons pertaining to physical conditions (e.g., diabetics, or those with high blood pressure or emphysema); others for moral reasons (e.g., Jews who keep kosher, or vegetarians who don't eat meat because they don't believe in killing animals); still others are cautious about what they eat because they want to improve their overall health (e.g., cholesterol-free or sugar-free diets).

I was a righteous and uncompromising vegetarian for years until one summer when I was working in Mexico. My hosts, an extremely poor family, had slaughtered their only chicken in honor of the *Cinco de Mayo* feast and to honor my friend and I who were attending. Seeing the look on their faces when I told them that I wouldn't eat the chicken because I was a vegetarian should have been enough to make me cry. At the time I didn't cry *or* eat the chicken, and I seriously regret it now.

There are basically a few choices about how to handle dietary differences over the holidays:

---

2 *The New York Times*, Health and News Review Section, Jan 4. 1995.

1.) You can hold strictly to the discipline of your diet, which may be necessary, particularly if it sustains your physical health;

2.) You can eat what is served to you for the holiday, provided you can digest it, and realize that the world will not crumble because you ate a slice of roast beef or a piece of birthday cake.

3.) You can do a little of each.

Choose, but make it a conscious, thoughtful choice. The same options hold true if you adhere to a particular dietary practice and are hosting the holiday gathering. Whereas a kosher family is probably not going to serve non-kosher foods in their home, a family that does not eat sugar or salt in their food may want to consider having these items available. Be sensitive to the dietary needs of your guests.

No matter what you need or may suspect that your family member needs, don't wait until dinner is set out on the table to address dietary differences. Make provisions ahead of time. When visiting, most of your hosts will not be insulted if you bring along a large gourmet vegetarian dish, or sugar-free brownies, for everybody to share. But discuss it ahead of time. If you are visiting a kosher home and need some bacon, or find you're in a vegetarian home and you need a hamburger, quietly take a drive to town in the afternoon and indulge your craving there. Be creative, and caring.

OVEREATING

Ninety-five percent of the articles in the holiday issues of popular magazines focus on the issue of overeating. Titles such as: "How to Have a Fat-Free Holiday," or "Christmas on 1500 Calories or Less" are commonly found on magazine covers. We care about how we look, and many of us *agonize* over holiday weight gain to such a degree that it can actually ruin a holiday. Even those of us who aren't calorie-conscious often find ourselves with heartburn, indigestion, and frustration at the inability to moderate food intake at holiday times.

> *Every year I bake my signature Christmas cookies while taking a vow not to eat my own or anybody else's. Meanwhile, the people I am baking for are making the same vows. Who is supposed to eat those cookies?!*

Unfortunately, there is almost always a grandmother or an aunt who will positively insist that you eat a fourth helping of mashed potatoes, or a third piece of pumpkin pie, placing it on your still-full plate in spite of your earnest protests. Then there are the rest of us who can manage stuffing ourselves just fine *sans* coercion.

A Few Hints For A Balanced Holiday Diet:

- Generally speaking, *err on the side of moderation with an extra tablespoon of indulgence.* Don't set yourself up with unreasonable expectations, but on the other hand, know what foods make you sick *every time* you eat them, and consider *that* before you reach for them.

- *If you're going to be snacking throughout the day, make a point to eat less during main meals.*

- *Try not to eat a big meal after 8 p.m. (no later than 6 would be ideal).* Food is processed more slowly during the evening and during sleep.

- *Regular exercise,* even if it is only a brisk fifteen-minute walk, *will speed up your metabolism,* burning off extra calories as a side-effect.

- *Eat fresh fruits and vegetables as snacks.* They are filling and healthy, loaded with enzymes and will keep you away from the candy bowl and the cookie jar.

- *Alcohol is highly caloric.* Most people don't count the calories in mixed drinks, but they quickly add up.

- *Digestive enzymes, available at all health food stores, aid in processing food quickly* and help the body to convert excess substances into usable nourishment. (I like to use Vitase™ Digestion Formula from Prevail Corporation).

- *Keep in mind that one of the main purposes of eating together is to nourish relationship.* So, if one of your goals is not to overeat, try eating a light meal while focusing instead on enjoying the company around the breakfast table.

PHYSICAL AND EMOTIONAL HEALTH

There is a direct link between physical and emotional health. Colds and flu abound during the holidays, and most of us will immediately go to the pharmacy for symptom relief medication without considering the emotional climate that may be at the root of weakened physical health.

According to Lalitha Thomas, popular author and lecturer on the relationship between mental health and the body, emotions of a pleasurable nature catalyze a positive immune-system response that supports good health. If you are happy to see your family, and they are glad to see you, this mood of love triggers an extraordinary brain chemistry that is vital to good health. Thomas reports cases of people who are sick before the holidays, but who, in the company of loving family, are brought to sudden health–or "loved alive," a term she coined.

> *My crotchety, old Mom virtually turns into a goddess of a grandmother when we bring the kids for Hanukkah. They adore her. Her asthma disappears and she's prancing around the kitchen without her walker, baking cookies with the kids and telling them stories during their bedtime snack.*

On the flip side, feelings of anxiety and the tense confrontations with family members that are common during the holidays have a strong degenerative effect on physical health. There are mechanisms in the physical body that correspond to tension, low self-esteem, and negative emotions, resulting in a physical chemistry that is health-negative. This physical/chemical response is heightened during the holidays because of many stress factors including gift giving, family expectations, and the American myth of "never be alone during the holidays." "The holidays are a higher stress stimuli than a full day on the subway," Thomas commented, "and can quickly deteriorate an immune system that is otherwise functioning fine."

Five Common Sense Considerations For A Healthy Holiday:

1.) *Drink lots of water.* As simple as this may sound, drinking lots of pure water is probably the healthiest form of preventive medicine you can practice. Most of us drink little water at family gatherings (unless it is mixed with instant coffee, or in the form of scotch and soda). Water keeps the body flushed and purified of smoke, alcohol, and additives (such as Red Dye #2 which is the main ingredient in those maraschino cherries in your fruitcakes). Drinking enough water also helps to handle temporary constipation that may accompany eating heavily, indulging in unique foods or sitting for long periods of time in one position.

2.) *Realize that different foods affect your emotions.* Sugar, red meat, caffeine, and other substances have a strong effect on the emotions. It's not that you shouldn't eat them, but if you're feeling suddenly emotional, reactive, or depressed, realize that it *may not* be your mother's incessant nagging. It may just be the food. Be particularly attentive to avoid taking these particular foods in great quantities. The additional stress on your system trying to process extra sugar, red meat, and caffeine is hard on your physical body as well as your emotional "body."

3.) *Get plenty of rest.* When you are overtired, as many of us are by the time we finally get to the wedding or anniversary celebration, common sense blurs, tempers rise, and emotions reign. Jet lag, time zone differences and sleeping in a strange bed can all contribute to fatigue. Keep the battery recharged—even a ten-minute nap can work wonders!

4.) *Exercise is a must.* Even if it is freezing outside and there is a foot of snow on the ground, if you have a specific discipline around exercise, don't stop now. Exercise is vital during holiday times to help stay strong and supple, to process excess food, as well as to create an outlet for emotional tension and stress. If you don't exercise, now is an excellent time to begin, gently, with a brisk stroll around the neighborhood every day. Or, treat yourself to a visit to a local health club.

5.) *Don't make promises that you can't keep.* Be disciplined but not rigid. If you have health guidelines, make an effort to stick to them while at your family's house or while your guests are visiting. Don't set yourself up for failure, though. You certainly don't have to stick to your "no sugar" rule on Christmas, and you may not have time to exercise every single day of your trip. Be reasonable with yourself.

If You Have Tried All Of The Above
And Your Emotions Are Still Running The Show:

- *Call a friend* who is outside of the family structure. Sometimes you just need to chat for a few minutes with somebody who is not involved in the family dynamic. You don't even have to talk about your family, or the difficulties of the family gathering. The connection with an understanding friend is healing in itself.

- *Take a break.* Give your emotions some breathing room. You are not obliged to spend every waking moment with your parents or your children. Go for a walk, take yourself out to coffee, have a long, hot bath, or do whatever it takes to have a little free space; maybe just take time to read the newspaper.

- *Put your face in a pillow and let out a loud scream, or have a good cry.* Pent up emotions don't usually disappear just because you are ignoring them. If your emotions are overflowing, it's better to take them out on a pillow than on your parent, sibling or child.

- *Be gentle with yourself.* Strong emotions are a sign of inner turmoil. Therefore, be kind to yourself by refusing to be self-critical, by taking it easy, and by doing things for yourself that help you to relax. Consider what advice you would give to a friend who is having a stressful time. Then, take your own advice.

- *Take a deep breath.* If you are willing to take thirty seconds (even five will do) to lie down and breathe deeply, there will be a shift in your mood.

•••

Knowing why the holidays are such a big deal, *understanding* family psychology and the holidays, and *being wise* about your health are the foundations for any successful family get-together. The following chapters address special "gathering" circumstances, such as funerals and family crisis situations; and specific concerns within some families—including gay and lesbian issues, the needs of young children (and their parents), and religious issues connected with the holidays.

4

When The "Holiday" Is A Family Crisis

*When the phone rang in the middle of the
night, I knew Dad had died. Even though he
had been in the hospital for three months, that
"call" ... the reality of his death ... shocked me
deeply. We all made plans to fly back home
the following day.*

Families get together for weddings and funerals, but
the moods of the occasions are vastly different. New survival rules apply when the family gathering is caused by a
sudden death, or the desire to support a loved one in their
last days of life, or to help with the institutionalization or
hospitalization of a family member. Sometimes it is a
would-be joyful occasion, such as an anniversary or

Mother's Day, only the person with whom you've always shared it is no longer alive, or is present but in an advanced stage of a terminal illness. At times like these, grief becomes the common link connecting family members.

Elisabeth Kubler-Ross defines the stages of grief that the dying person, as well as his or her loved ones, pass through as: denial, anger, bargaining, depression, and acceptance.[3] These five stages of grief apply equally to all forms of loss, great and small, whether it be the first family reunion after Jeff's death, or the surprise anniversary party that is given prior to an impending divorce. You might also be grieving something or "someone" who never lived at all, as when you suffer the disintegration of a long-held illusion about your family (e.g., the realization that your family is *not* the Waltons).

> *My sister Sandy refused to come to my baby shower because she recently had a miscarriage. I told her that I understood, but in fact I felt deeply saddened by her choice.*

Sandy was grieving, and because of her pain she made a choice that offended her sister. Intoxicated by her own joy and excitement at the upcoming birth of her child,

---

3 Kubler-Ross, Elisabeth. *On Death and Dying.* New York: MacMillan, 1969.

—When The "Holiday" Is A Family Crisis—

Sandy's sister failed to appreciate how devastating the grief of a miscarriage was. We are all products of a grief-denying culture which expects people to be over and done with their pain as soon as possible, at least before the next family event or the next holiday season. While Sandy could have opted to ask a close friend to come to the baby shower with her, as an understanding companion, or chosen to have come for only a short while, her decision to skip the whole event was more likely a necessary and beneficial choice to support her grieving process.

Grief is work. (Freud called the integration of grief, "grief work.") When something significant is lost, there are thousands of details of everyday life (to which that something or someone was connected) that have to be acknowledged, mourned and then integrated. This can be quite a labor.

Grief also takes time. Even if the person for whom you grieve is still alive, as when a child gets divorced or an aged parent loses their memory, grief can be long-term and extremely painful. Earlier psychological theories suggested that eight to nine months would be sufficient time to bring people functionally back to normal after a significant loss. However, contemporary psychological thinking suggests that it can take three to four years after a loss before a person feels like himself or herself again.[4]

---

4 A more detailed description of how to open up to grief can be found in *When Sons and Daughters Choose Alternative Lifestyles*, (Hohm Press, 1996) pp. 50-52.

My grandfather died three years ago. Since then Hanukkah has not been the same. We still light the candles and exchange gifts but it is suddenly empty. My father tries to take over leading the rituals, but it doesn't work. My grandfather had been the passion behind the celebration. I feel very disillusioned with the holidays. My love for Hanukkah seems to have died with my grandfather.

IMPORTANT REMINDERS FOR FAMILY CRISIS SITUATIONS:

- *If there has been a death in the family, the first round of holidays following the transition is the period of the most significant grief.* Give yourself extra time to mourn. It is not wise to rush the process.

- *Grief shows up in many ways*—sometimes in the body (e.g., teeth grinding, ulcers, diminished/excess appetite), sometimes in the mind (e.g., disturbed thoughts and fantasies, dullness), and through the emotions (roller coaster feelings, fits of anger or bouts of crying). In other words, if your brother Jack drops some snide comment on the Thanksgiving following your mother's death that, "Mom always overcooked the turkey anyway," he is probably just going through the grieving stage of anger. Be patient with him by not criticizing him for his rude comment.

- *There will be unanticipated reactions in family members during times of grief,* ranging from withdrawal, numbness and depression, to unusual expressions of joy and inappropriate laughter. If you can see these behaviors as recognizable manifestations of grief, you can let others be, neither judging them nor comparing yourself to them.

- *Children will also be affected by grief, even if you may think they are too young to understand what is going on.* Although children are incredibly resilient, and their holiday enthusiasm will still be present, their inner stability is largely at the effect of those around them. Their grief may show up as regressive behaviors (bedwetting) or acting out (temper tantrums). Give them an opportunity to regress without embarrassing them or withdrawing your love and support. Help foster an atmosphere of understanding and affection.

- *Depending upon the severity of the loss, people may feel crazy or disoriented when grieving.* They may have difficulties making simple everyday decisions such as what to eat or what to wear.

- *Guilt and self-blame go hand-in-hand.* Let go of the burden that you could have prevented the crisis, whatever it was, or that you are somehow to blame for it. None of us are prophets or saviors. Acknowledge to yourself that you're doing the best you can.

DON'T IGNORE THE ELEPHANT IN THE MIDDLE OF THE ROOM

> *My whole family went to the hospital on New Year's Day to visit Tony, my brother who was dying of AIDS. Everybody was talking happy-talk about what a lovely snow we had, and how wonderful it was that my sister was getting married. Nobody said to Tony, "How are you coming along?" or, "Is there anything you'd like to talk about with me?"*

The elephant in the middle of Tony's hospital room was so massive that his trunk was sticking out the window. Yet nobody said a word about it to Tony. Some of us do not address the grief at hand because we are afraid to. We feel awkward and don't know what to do. Others deny their grief because they don't want their holidays to be spoiled–they feel entitled to their "white Christmas" and they don't want anybody messing with it. For those who would like to take a shot at the elephant, facing these awkward and often threatening moments with awareness and compassion, here are a few helpful suggestions.

Three Ways To Acknowledge The Elephant In The Middle Of The Room:

1.) *Make a pointed but sensitive statement or ask a question to determine how open others are to talking straight.* After establishing a caring rapport, Elizabeth Kubler-Ross used to ask a dying patient: "How sick are you?" If the person said, "I'm doing great and I can't wait to go home," she would follow that lead and continue talking about less confrontive topics. On the other hand, such a question proved an invaluable opener for those who needed to talk about their fears and anguish. At a family gathering where the elephant is looming large, one might comment or question along similar lines.

2.) *Tell the story of your own grief,* again and again. If most others are uncomfortable talking about the loss, find someone who isn't and sequester yourself with them for awhile.

3.) *When somebody else wants to tell you the story of their grief, listen.* This may bring up painful feelings or discomfort, but it is a necessary part of the grieving process for you and for them. Each person must grieve in their own time. Make *your* peace with it, and stay available by actively listening for any opportunity to meet them halfway, when *they* are ready.

Those who are close to dying can sustain themselves to fulfill short-term holiday goals. Researchers David Phillips and Kenneth Feldman documented a decline in the death rate immediately before such occasions as religious events, birthdays and national holidays, even among people with terminal disease. These statistics represent a temporary postponement of an inevitability.[5] Therefore, it is important for you not to misconstrue a loved one's sudden change in health or willfulness as a remission or permanent turn in their condition, thereby slipping into your own denial of the situation.

Holidays *can* bring about miracles, but reality remains reality, and none of us has a crystal ball to foresee the future. Not long ago, for instance, a close family friend was dying of cancer, but was holding out for a break in his chemotherapy schedule so he could visit his first grandson who had been born in Asia. Despite the seriousness of his condition, everybody else in the family had convinced themselves that he would make it to Japan, and they were all shocked when his health took a sudden turn for the worse, and he died without making the trip.

---

5 Phillips, D.P., & Feldman, K.A. (1973) A dip in deaths before ceremonial occasions: Some new relationships between social integration and mortality. *American Sociological Review, 38*, p. 678.

AN OPPORTUNITY FOR DEEPENING

Pain is an important part of life. We grow and deepen through our suffering. Death, illness and crisis present a chance to come into a more honest relationship with ourselves and those we love. When people are thrown off balance by an emergency, it is as if somebody has pulled the rug out from underneath them; the humdrum of their ordinary lives is suddenly interrupted resulting in a crack in their ordinary perception. This crack is an opening, and within it exists the opportunity to come closer to one's self and to others.

My mother's funeral was one of the few times when I saw my father really crying. It felt right to be able to put my hand on his shoulder and support him—our parent/child separation was temporarily set aside.

Three Suggestions For Greater Closeness:

1.) *Allow yourself to feel and express your pain.* If you need to be alone and the house is full of guests, go someplace and let yourself cry. Or plan for a walk to a secluded spot and bring a large handkerchief.

2.) *Take the risk of expressing your feelings to others.* In doing so, you will find a sweetness to your sorrow, and you may discover things you never knew about those around you.

3.) *Create a family ritual in which the grief can be shared* —like a prayer service or a ceremonial family visit to the grave of the deceased person.

SOME PRACTICAL ADVICE FOR SURVIVING THE FAMILY CRISIS SANELY:

- *Pack your emotional suitcase.* Add special artifacts–photos, books of poetry, or music that soothes you–to your bag.

- *Pamper yourself.* Bring along some bubble bath, or bake some chocolate chip cookies and keep them handy.

- *Set up a support team.* Make a commitment *in advance* to call your therapist (if you have one) at least once while you're visiting your family, and/or to call a friend back home every day. Committing to this in advance will insure you a link to the outside world if you start to get lost in the mire of emotions of the family gathering.

- *Take time out.* Go for a walk in the park, out to a coffee shop, or take time to see a movie to gain a little perspective and breathing space.

—When The "Holiday" Is A Family Crisis—

- *Bring a writing journal.* Use it to help access your inner wisdom, or simply to draw, doodle or write letters to yourself.

- *Stay healthy.* Health is an important aspect of emotional stability. Eat well, get plenty of rest, and be sure to drink lots of water.

- *Physical movement is very helpful in processing grief.* Find activities that take you back down to earth: walking, vacuuming the house, weeding the garden, shoveling snow, moving rocks or transplanting trees. Grief gets processed through the body, so keeping your body active will allow the grief cycle to move through you more completely.

- *Consider bringing along a friend* who knows you well and can support you.

- *Take refuge in your religious faith or spiritual practice.*

- *Engage creativity.* It is an excellent way to handle grief. Write, paint, draw, cook, play music, dance.

- *Remember:* This too shall pass.

5

When It Comes To Chilren & Grandchildren

Holidays can be particularly stressful to kids. Although children often delight in family gatherings and can extract the essence of them in a way that adults may have lost, stress remains. Kids have their own anxieties about many things that adults often fail to appreciate. They may be anxious simply in terms of getting the gifts they want, or more significantly in negotiating their way through the masses of known and unknown family and friends, foods and environments. All this is compounded by the fact that they will absorb (and often act out) the anxiety of others, and of the culture itself, which inadvertently affects them. Therefore, it is the responsibility of the adults in a child's environment to be especially sensitive to children's needs. In the first part of this chapter I will speak to the parents of young children who are trying to navigate their way through the holiday visit. Later, I will address grandparents who are faced with the relationship not only to their grandchildren, but to their children who are now parents as well.

FOR PARENTS WITH CHILDREN:

> *My mom was chasing my four-year-old son Bobby around the living room: "Don't you want to put on this nice green and red Christmas outfit instead of having dinner in your underwear and T-shirt?" "Don't you want to make Grannie proud of you in front of all the relatives?" Yet Bobby would not hear of it.*

Bobby had been raised with his boundaries respected; he wasn't about to budge for Granny's eccentric whim. Parenting styles often differ dramatically between grandparents and parents. While it can be wonderful to see your children with your parents (you may see a fun-loving and caring side of your folks that is often unavailable), on the other hand, you may find yourself feeling critical or uncomfortable with how your parents or other relatives respond to your children.

A Few Hints For Parents:

* *Be prepared and plan ahead,* particularly in the following areas:
  * ❋ *Length of stay.* Do you want to spend every day with your folks, or would it be better to spend part of the time with them and then take a small holiday with just your children?
  * ❋ *Sleeping arrangements.* Do you anticipate problems in terms of housing or being housed by your family? For example, is the fact that your two-year-old still shares a bed with you distasteful to your hosts? Will your parents find it too difficult to share a bathroom with their six grandkids? If you make arrangements ahead of time, your guests or hosts will appreciate your consideration.
  * ❋ *Traveling.* It is unreasonable to expect a four-year-old to sit through a ten-hour car ride with bathroom breaks at two-hour intervals. Travel can be stressful for children. You may not realize how stressed they are until they react with upset stomachs or diarrhea, or when they wet their beds long after they have been potty-trained.

✳ *Food.* Will your children's dietary needs be adequately tended to at your destination and along the way? To ease the stress, you can bring foods that your kids are familiar with, and be prepared to cook meals they are used to if the menu doesn't suit them.

• *Give your parents or other family relations a little slack in terms of both their parenting style around your children* and any attempts they may make at trying to change *your* parenting style. You've got to realize that to your own parents you will always be their child, and they're still going to try to show you how to do it their way. As with other adult relatives, be patient and keep your sense of humor.

• *Be willing to set boundaries with your parents or others for the sake of your children.* If you do not normally feed your children sugar, you don't have to allow grandma to give them treats ten times a day. The art of compromise is a wonderful skill to cultivate.

• *Bring games and crafts along for your children to play with while traveling* and create planned activities while you are visiting.

• *Consider planning an outing with your own immediate family during an extended family visit*–particularly when the tension is rising. Even a walk in the woods or a rousing game of Monopoly can focus a family's attention together again.

- *Remember that your relationship with your parents (and brothers, sisters, aunts, and uncles) is your business, not your children's.* Be sure to communicate a compassionate stance to your children about your relatives, even if you don't feel it. You might choose to say, "That's just Aunt Betty's thing. She wants you to kiss everybody goodnight before you go to bed, but you don't have to," instead of complaining, "Aunt B. has always been a controlling and manipulative nag. Just ignore her and forget the kisses."

- *Realize that your parents or other family members may not treat your kids the same way they treated you as a child*–don't box them into old expectations. The holiday visit is not the time to address old wounds and hurt feelings.

    It's the most amazing thing. When we surprised my parents with a visit on Grandparent's Day, I was so uptight when my little girl flung food all over the place from her highchair. That was completely forbidden when I was growing up, but they didn't mind at all! Were these the

> *same people who had raised me—these people*
> *who had suddenly become the epitome of mel-*
> *lowness and had relaxed all rules in the hope*
> *that their granddaughter might sit on their laps?*

• *Let your parents spoil their grandchildren for a few*
days a year, if spoiling is giving them a few extra treats,
lots of attention, and healthy affection. Grandparents
offer their grandchildren a unique relationship. Allow it to
grow.

FOR GRANDPARENTS WITH CHILDREN AND GRANDCHILDREN:

> *I thought my daughter was going a little bit*
> *overboard when she wouldn't let my nine-year-*
> *old granddaughter go to midnight Mass with us*
> *because she was afraid the child would want to*
> *stay up that late all the time. By the time you're*
> *a grandparent, you see how rigid parents can*
> *sometimes be with their children.*

Grandparents often have a broader and wiser perspective that parents sometimes don't have. The holiday challenge is to enjoy your grandchildren to the fullest, while
honoring your own children's parenting styles.

A Few Hints For Grandparents And Other Senior Relatives:

- *Be prepared.* Whether the whole family is coming to your home, or you're going to be with your children and grandchildren at theirs, plan ahead. As stated above in the parent's section, pay special attention to the following:
  - ❋ *Length of stay.* You are not obliged to make your house into a hotel for the whole extended family for two weeks, unless you want to. Make wise choices about the appropriate length of time to visit or to have visitors.
  - ❋ *Sleeping arrangements.* If they are coming to your house, ask them what works best. If you're going to be visiting them, decide if it would be better to stay with the family or to stay at a hotel.
  - ❋ *Food.* If you don't know what your nieces and nephews or grandchildren like to eat for breakfast, or if your children and their family frequently change diets, find out their preferences ahead of time and stock up.

- *Don't try to teach your children how to be parents.* Your children are still your children, but they are also adults and parents. (And you won't be able to change their parenting style in a week-long visit anyway.)

- *You can set boundaries with your children and your grandchildren.* You needn't let them jump on the couch or dig for worms in your rose garden.

- *Have games available for your nieces and nephews or grandchildren,* and plan activities like as cookie-bakes, cook-outs, hikes, and bike rides with them.

- *Go on a date with your husband or wife or a friend during a lengthy visit.* You don't have to put your relationships on hold just because it is the holidays and you have company.

- *Remember that your relationship with your son or daughter is your business, not your grandchild's.* Be a role model of understanding and patience with your children, for the sake of your grandchildren.

PRESENTS OR PRESENCE?

> *My sister and her husband are recently divorced, and their seven-year-old son wants to spend time with his father. But he's so busy working all the time to make money to buy special presents for the boy, that he won't set aside a weekend to just be with him.*

Presence is worth more than *presents,* though there is space for both. Children learn greed when gifts replace authenticity. Holidays are an opportunity to practice the principles you stand for, which is a greater gift for your child than training him in the sciences of avarice and consumerism.

Yet, gifts are a very sensitive issue for children. Because holidays–particularly the winter holidays of Christmas and Hanukkah–have such a large focus on materialism, parents, grandparents and relatives feel an enormous pressure to keep up with this momentum, even if they cannot afford to. They want to give their kids and grandkids the things *they* never had; they want to feel that they are good parents and grandparents; they don't want the kids to have to show up at school on January 2nd with nothing to talk about at Show-and-Tell.

> *My son and daughter-in-law have a child who is two. My daughter-in-law has a very large family which is big into gifts. The two-year-old got about seventy-five presents all at once this Christmas. She was completely overwhelmed in the hysteria of just ripping wrapping paper off packages. They wisely decided that next year they would give her just a couple of gifts on Christmas Eve and a few for her to open on Christmas day.*

The whole gift ordeal is so taxing that some parents would rather forget about it altogether. A co-worker of mine told me about one large family she worked with who couldn't always afford to buy a substantial gift for each of their children on the holidays. One year the parents considered giving no gifts at all, but they knew that would cause tremendous upset for the kids and guilt for themselves. Their creative solution required courage–they asked several of their wealthier relatives to each buy a gift for one of the children. The risk paid off. The relatives were more than happy to do it, and everybody was pleased in the end.

A Few Final Ideas On Gift-Giving And Children:

- *When it come to gifts and mixed families, pay special attention not to show favoritism.* If there are children, step-children, and step-grandchildren at the gathering, be sensitive to their needs. Buy gifts of relatively equal value, or ones that can be shared, such as a sled, a trampoline, or a group game.

- *Don't use gifts as a weapon.* You don't have to *buy* your children or grandchildren's love to outdo your ex-husband or ex-wife, to assuage your guilt, or to compensate for not seeing your children or grandchildren all year long.

• *Plan a group outing that includes everybody,* such as a trip to the park, a basketball game, or an afternoon of ice skating. "Unique adventures" as gifts will be remembered for many years.

As we close this chapter, here are a few additional points to remember:

✳ Watch your language around the holidays. Young children take things literally. When Uncle Mike sits three-year-old Johnny on his lap and says, "If you're not a good little boy between now and Christmas, Santa is going to fly right over your house and not come in," Johnny believes him. Lacking the capacity for adult discrimination, children absorb impressions like a sponge. It is your obligation as a parent or as a grandparent to do the discerning for them.

✳ Try to anticipate your child's needs or be willing to alter plans in mid-stream if necessary, for *their* comfort.

✳ Offering your *presence* rather than or in addition to *presents*, embodies the true spirit of the holidays.

✳ Where children or grandchildren, nieces and nephews are concerned, approach the holiday with as few expectations

as possible, yet be prepared for unexpected scenarios to
arise.

6

Don We Now Our Gay (And Lesbian) Apparel, FaLaLaLaLa...

Whether you are gay, lesbian or bisexual,[1] *or* you are the parent, child, sibling or relative of somebody who is, issues around homosexuality and the family peak during the holiday season, with discomfort, uncertainty and insecurity all coming out of the closet. I have divided this chapter into two parts in order to address both sides of the situation. In the first part I will consider the possible scenarios that the gay person might face when it comes to holidays, and in the second part I will discuss the family gathering from the perspective of the family of the gay individual.

---

6 For purposes of simplicity I will use the term "gay" throughout the chapter to include all of the various sexual identities.

The following conversation occurred between a caller and the host of the National Public Radio broadcast I heard in San Francisco:

Caller: *I'm the partner of somebody who has just come out to his parents, and we're going to his folk's house for the first time. What should I be thinking about before we go?*
Talk show host: *You mean you're the very first boyfriend he's ever brought home?"*
Caller: *Yes.*
Talk show host: *You're a gutsy soul!*

Bringing your partner home for the family gathering for the first time can be a very awkward and potentially stressful situation. *Homophobia,* a term coined by George Weinberg in *Society and the Healthy Homosexual,* refers to the fear of being in close quarters with homosexuals.[7] This fear of homosexuality can be subtle or overt, but it permeates the cultural mind. Whether you are gay, lesbian or bisexual there are no *easy* answers.

IF YOU ARE GAY, LESBIAN OR BISEXUAL

When I came home for the holidays one year, I decided to tell my father I was gay. All of a

---

7 Weinberg, George. *Society and the Healthy Homosexual.* Boston, MA: Alyson Publications, 1991, p. 4.

> *sudden he was acting like he was having a heart attack, and started crying out, "I'm dying. How can I live?" Of course he lived—it was just a big drama. But just before Christmas Mass he approached me and said, "I know this gay-thing is a phase you're going through, so we're all going to pray for you to get better."*
>
> *"Pray 'cause you need to pray," I said, "but getting better, for me, is not the point."*

Homosexuality is not widely accepted and understood in our society. Responses range from full acceptance to a politically-correct, pseudo-acceptance of homosexuality, to an outright rejection and denial of homosexuality. The point of the holidays is to celebrate with your loved ones, not to make a political protest. Although your family may be prejudiced or ignorant about gay issues, the burden will fall on you to create a holiday that is not only tolerable, but that is enjoyable as well.

What To Do And What Not to Do For A Sane Holiday:

Generally speaking ...

- *Don't assume you know how somebody will react to your sexual orientation.* Some people who you think will be homophobic will be surprisingly accepting and

non-reactive; others who you imagine will be supportive, will create a nightmare. One man I know was convinced his boyfriend's mother would reject him outright. Instead, as soon as he walked off the plane she
greeted him smiling and with a kiss on the cheek.

- *Realize that your family's reactions to you may not be
  because you are gay.* They may just be the responses
  of a normal neurotic family. Try not to jump to conclusions.

- *Remember: Coming out is a moment-to-moment process.*

- *Don't wait for your family's attitude to change to have a
  special holiday.* If your family is not supportive, accept
  their inability to accept you, and do the best you can
  with what you've got.

- *Recognize that your parents have to acknowledge and
  accept that they have a gay child too,* and that over a
  Thanksgiving dinner, surrounded by distant relatives,
  may not be the time they wish to talk about it. Think of
  how long it took you to come out to yourself and to others; it may take just as long for your parents. Be
  patient with their process–things are more likely to
  change over time.

- *As long as they are kind to you, let your family's judgments be* their *problem.*

- *If your family really has a problem with you being gay, and hassles you about it every time you visit, don't spend the holidays with them.* Find some friends to celebrate with, instead of visiting your family. Many gay people create wonderful extended families within the gay community.

Before the visit ...

- *Don't wait until ten o'clock on Christmas Eve to bring up the sleeping arrangements.* Make plans in advance. If they want your boyfriend or girlfriend to sleep in the guest room, decide if you are willing to make that compromise. It may be far simpler for you both to stay at a hotel.

- *Make a decision about being out to each of your family members before you go to visit* and stay with your decision, unless an unexpected circumstance should arise. Don't be subtle or sneaky.

- *If you are going home with a partner, discuss in advance together how you're going to approach the situation* in terms of talking about being gay, or showing physical affection with one another.

- *If you do plan to come out to them over the holidays, have support ready for your family.* PFLAG (Parents, Friends and Families of Lesbians and Gays) has a national support network throughout the country. The national office can be reached at (202) 638-4200. Have this number and some literature available for them and give your family *time* to assimilate the news.

During the visit ...

- *Focus on common interests.* One man I spoke with found out that he shared a love of classical music and good wine with his boyfriend's mother, so he brought her several of his favorite CDs and they spent most of Passover evening listening to music and drinking wine together.

- *Reassure them that there's more to you than being gay.* To you it's obvious, but your family may need to be reminded. If you love to cook, join the folks in the kitchen, or if sports is your passion, watch the Super Bowl with those glued to the tube.

- *Be sensitive to your partner's needs as well as your own,* if you are going to your parents' home with a lover. Be particularly considerate if you are not out to your family and are going to visit your folks but leaving your partner behind.

- *Be careful of the desire to shock your family.* There is a fine line between being political out of anger, and being political out of love. Be wary of using the family holiday as a time to make major political statements.

- *Find out what the gay/lesbian resources are in town.* Sometimes if you can just go out to a gay bookstore or a gay coffee shop for an hour you'll be recharged and ready to return to the family hearth.

- *Remember to affirm yourself.* You are who you are, but this can be difficult to remember when you're constantly being questioned and doubted by those around you. Practically speaking, this may mean bringing a gay novel along to read before you go to bed at night, or telephoning somebody from your community back home to remind you who you are.

- *Remember that you don't need your family's approval to sustain an excellent relationship with your gay partner.* You are an adult and have made an adult decision.

- *Take a walk with your lover at least once a day* if you are home for the holidays with them. Or go out for dessert. Do something in which you can be alone as a couple in order to reestablish your connection as lovers, and to give yourselves time to discuss what is going on. It is easy to get lost in the flood of conscious and unconscious emotions that surges through the family holiday. One lesbian couple I spoke with agreed that the most challenging aspect of family visits is that they don't feel comfortable showing physical affection with one another in the presence of their families, and that by the time they get back to their own home they feel like neighbors instead of lovers.

- *Watch how normal it can be.* If you are convinced that the whole holiday will be full of tension and awkward moments, you may find yourself surprised to realize how much they *do* accept you, and *do* see you for who you are.

IF SOMEBODY YOU KNOW IS GAY

The holidays can be challenging for both the family and friends of the gay individual. For most people, "knowing someone gay" usually connotes a relationship with a son or a daughter, a business colleague or a friend. Lately, however, I've been hearing many stories from younger adults about parents or other relatives who have come out of the closet; a situation which poses its own unique challenges.

Perhaps you are comfortable with your family member's gayness but are concerned that your narrow-minded sister will offend someone by making a prejudiced slur. Or maybe it dawns on you in a flash that the lovely young woman your sister has been bringing home with her for years is actually her mate. Maybe you want to make your gay family member feel comfortable in your house but you don't know how to talk to them about it, or maybe you don't *want* them to feel extremely comfortable because you would rather have them stay in a hotel.

One thirty-year-old woman shared the following story:

> *For thirty-two years, my father hid the fact that he was gay from my mom. He didn't tell anybody because we lived in Oklahoma and the word "gay" didn't even exist there. The last Christmas I spent with my parents together, I could feel that something was terribly wrong. My mother was worried about their relationship so she got him a wedding ring for Christmas to reinstate their vows. He made it clear that he disliked the gift, and we were all left to wonder what was going on.*

As the story goes, the father ran away to San Francisco with his gay lover a few weeks later, and the mother eventually remarried. But at the time of the holiday in question, this family was confused. Unfortunately, it did not cross anyone's mind to actually *talk* together to ease the situation.

On a radio interview I did over the past holiday season, a middle-aged business man called me up panicked that he was going to have a breakdown because his son had just made an "irrational and immoral" decision. Upon further questioning, he proceeded to describe a young man who had turned to Satan worship and wanted to slaughter a chicken in front of the Christmas tree.

While I did not confront him directly, as a therapist I intuitively guessed that he was dealing with his son's gayness, which this man saw as equivalent to Satan worship or worse.

Whether you are in pain because your daughter has just come out to you, or if you are struggling about how to come out to other relatives about your mother's (child's or sibling's) gayness, just remember that the holidays don't have to be the time when all issues get addressed. Holiday gatherings should be about acceptance and hospitality, understanding and compassion.

What To Do And What Not To Do For A Sane Holiday:

Generally speaking...

- *Set up support for yourself.* It is important to realize that you are not alone and that there are many others who have felt confused, threatened or simply uncomfortable in learning that a family member was gay. PFLAG (Parents, Friends and Families of Lesbians and Gays) provides resources, literature and contacts for support groups in most major cities and towns. The national office can be reached at (202) 638-4200. You can attend meetings prior to the holiday visit, or arrange for a support person to be available by telephone during the holidays.

- *Don't take others' reactions to your family member's gayness personally.* Their reactions are *theirs.* It's not about you.

- *If you are nervous about using the correct language in speaking to the gay person* (for example, if you don't know what word to use to refer to his or her partner), *ask him or her for help.* Honesty and openness creates warmth, sincerity and a deeper bond in relationship.

- *Realize that the situation may be as difficult and awk-ward for them as it is for you.*

Before the visit ...

- *If you are going to be coming out to family and friends about your family member's gayness, practice in advance.* If you are comfortable with it, they will probably be more comfortable too. If you present such news as a tragedy, they are likely to hear it that way also.

- *Anticipate potential problems in advance,* and talk honestly with the gay individual about how you plan to handle these problems. For example, if it is important to you that your mother not know that John is your son's boyfriend, talk with him about it and work something out, instead of walking on eggshells all weekend, fearfully anticipating that he will come out to her.

During the visit ...

- *Treat a gay person like a normal person,* which is exactly what he or she is—he or she just happens to be gay! People often feel anxious about how to act around someone who is gay, forgetting that he or she is just another individual.

- *Take interest in the gay individual's life.* There is more to him or her than sexual orientation. A gay man from a large extended family told me that the hardest part of the holidays is when everybody sits around for hours after dinner talking about their lives, and the only thing they ask him is, "How's work?"

- *If your gay family member has come home with a partner, acknowledge him or her as such.* This can be awkward and embarrassing for many people. One woman, whose mother is quite open and accepting of her (the daughter's) lesbian lifestyle, told me, "My Mom always calls us 'the girls,' and introduces us as 'my daughters.' We have to constantly remind her, 'Laurie is not your daughter, she is your daughter-*in-law*.' She appreciates the reminder."
  Not everybody can be as liberal as this mother, certainly, but everybody can be kind and sensitive in not ignoring the new partner.

- *If you know your gay family member has a partner, ask him or her about that person,* just as you would if he or she had a heterosexual partner. One man said to me, "If somebody would just ask me, 'How's Mike?' I would be so grateful. They don't even have to say the dreaded word *boyfriend*. If they could just ask that one thing I would feel included in the holiday celebration."

- *If some family member has surprised you by coming out to you over the holidays, don't panic, over-react, or jump to conclusions.* Strong feelings are natural, and you may go through a grieving process, but you don't have to outwardly express all your negative feelings. Keep in mind that this person is still the same one you've known all along.

If we allow each person in our family—whether gay, lesbian, bisexual, heterosexual, divorced, remarried, separated, adult, teenager, child—the same freedom of expression that we would give to any of our friends, the spirit of holidays or family gatherings can nourish and expand our relationships rather than diminish and constrict them.

7

Keeping The Faith:
For Those With
Spiritual Concerns

America is essentially a Judeo-Christian culture, with few other religions or spiritual beliefs receiving any wide recognition and acceptance. For those of us outside of this cultural milieu, the holidays can be taxing. Similarly, those who strongly adhere to their Jewish or Christian faith, and have family members who *do not,* may experience discomfort, embarrassment and conflict over the holidays. This chapter will provide helpful hints for those on both sides. In the first part, I will look at the holidays from the perspective of the individual involved in a non-traditional religion or spiritual practice. Later, I will discuss how it is from the perspective of the family members of the individual who has an alternative spiritual or religious practice.

Many years ago, in my rebellious stage, I made the acquaintance of a Native American shaman, or medicine man. It was during my first year of college (yes, the same year I refused to eat the turkey at Thanksgiving). I had invited this man over for a small birthday celebration. To my surprise, he began to burn sage–a purifying herb that smells much like marijuana–in the living room, and to chant traditional Mayan songs while pounding loudly on his deerskin drum. I could hardly contain my laughter imagining all-too-clearly the reactions of my older brother and his friends who were watching movies in the den. The next morning when my brother got up for work at 5 A.M. he stood outside my bedroom door beating on the bottom of a pot and letting loose an Indian war cry at the top of his lungs, to get me back.

IF YOU ARE A "NEW AGER," BUDDHIST, HINDU, ATHEIST, WITCH, YOGA PRACTITIONER, SOMEONE WHO HAS CONVERTED TO ANOTHER RELIGION OR IS INVOLVED IN AN INTERFAITH RELATIONSHIP, OR ANY ECLECTIC COMBINATION THEREOF ...

... the holidays will be a test of how truly enlightened (or unenlightened) you are.

> *My mother is Catholic and is terrified that she is*
> *going to end up in heaven and I won't be there*
> *because I don't go to Mass. She figures that*
> *she'll get in to the pearly gates and that I'll be*
> *locked out because she says the official prayers*
> *and I don't.*

All non-traditional spiritual orientations are certainly not the same, but in the eyes of some family members–unless you've got a pretty enlightened family–there is little difference whether you call yourself a "walk-in" from Venus or a Tibetan Buddhist. You've got to realize that although many Hollywood stars (yes, even they!) openly adhere to non-traditional spiritual practices, the growing popularity of such alternatives has only arisen within the past ten years. Many members of your family may have no paradigm in which to place your choices. They simply don't understand. So, you have two choices in terms of approaching the situation:

1.) You can try to integrate your spiritual practice or religion into your family's holiday;

2.) You can go along with their program, maintaining your own practices either behind closed doors or in the privacy of your own heart.

Some Helpful Reminders:

- *If your spiritual practice is what keeps you going, keep it alive during the visit.* Bring a small picture, prayer book, or poem to read every morning or evening that reminds you of your own spiritual path.

- *Understand it is hard for your family.* Religion embodies a way of life, and to them your choice to pursue an alternative to their religion, or to simply not observe any religious practices at all, is a rejection of their worldview. Therefore, please don't be surprised if you find you've generated some hurt feelings.

- *Be sensitive and discrete.* It is unnecessary to hang a picture of your guru on the Christmas tree, or to announce that you'll be out drinking at the local bar while everyone else is at midnight Mass. If it's difficult for your family members that you have become a devout Roman Catholic, and they are uncomfortable with you wearing a large crucifix around your neck, put it inside your shirt during family meals and do your praying in the guest room.

- *Keep a sense of humor!* There *is* something funny about trying to explain to your family why your boyfriend's name is Running Bull or, if you are a liberal Jew in a family of Orthodox Jews, why you allow your children to eat chocolate Santa Claus candies in December.

- *Remember, if the dinner table conversation is focused on what a shame it is that you are the only non-practicing Christian in your family,* skillfully turn the conversation toward the other family members, by asking questions. They'll be so grateful for a sympathetic ear that they may not even think about the fact that you're not living the life they think you should be living.

- *Talk to others about your spiritual orientation in a language they can understand.* If they say, "Amen," at the end of the meal prayer, and you say, "Hari Krishna," they're going to look at you like you've been abducted by an alien. If you have a tendency to shock, try to keep it at bay during the family gathering.

What not to say:

Mom, I've started hanging out with some Indian shamans. They're like medicine men and go around in loincloths, with feathers in their hair. There's this Sundance ceremony I went to where they pierce the guys' chests with these wooden pegs and hang them from a tree. It's really cool. They also smoke a lot — to them it's sacred, not like a drug or anything.

What to say:

Mom, I've become interested in Native American spirituality. It adds another dimension to my spiritual life. I've had some very pleasant and strong experiences at some of the rituals I have attended. It's quite fascinating.

- *If you are in an interfaith relationship, find compromises that work for you and your family.* One couple I spoke with visits the Jewish side of the family on Yom Kippur, spends Christmas Eve and Christmas morning with their own nuclear family, spends Christmas afternoon and the next few days with the Christian side of the family, and invites the whole extended family to their home for the Fourth of July.

- *Time is a great healer.* Your family will calm down once they see that you still love children, enjoy ice cream, and can appreciate a hot bath.

- *Model your spirituality instead of talking about it.* If you're a born-again Christian (or a Buddhist, or an orthodox Jew), the essence of your practice is about compassion and love. Be an example of that, and there may be no need for further explanation.

IF YOU ARE A FAMILY MEMBER OF A "NEW AGER," BUDDHIST, HINDU, ATHEIST, WITCH, YOGA PRACTITIONER, SOMEONE WHO HAS CONVERTED TO ANOTHER RELIGION OR IS INVOLVED IN AN INTERFAITH RELATIONSHIP, OR ANY ECLECTIC COMBINATION THEREOF ...

...the holidays will be a test of how patient and understanding you really are.

The whole family was sitting around eating birthday cake when my daughter told me she was going on a spiritual pilgrimage to India and was going to shave her head and pierce her nose in preparation. I thought I'd have a stroke!

What would you do if you quietly walked downstairs on Christmas Eve to place the gifts under the tree and your "pagan" daughter had set up a circle of black candles in front of the Christmas tree? Or if you are a devout Catholic, what would you say if your son and his Jewish wife asked you to participate in their baby son's *briss* at the local synagogue?

You have two options in your approach to your family member's non-traditional or differing faith spiritual practices:
1.) You can try to understand your family member's religious/spiritual choices and make room for them amidst your holiday celebration;
2.) You can acknowledge that you don't understand and even that you don't want to, without withdrawing your essential love and support of them as family members.

Some Helpful Reminders:

- *If your child is 15 - 21 years old, anticipate some rebellion.* If your church-going college-age daughter goes to Ft. Lauderdale over Christmas vacation instead of spending the holiday with the family, don't panic.

- On the other hand, *don't assume rebellion.* Your family member's religious experimentation may just be a phase he or she is going through, but it may not be. Do not discredit their perspective. It may not be defiant behavior. I know individuals whose parents have believed them to be "going through a phase" for the past twenty-five years.

- *Over-zealousness is common when people initially engage new spiritual practices.* If your child is preaching or trying to convert the family, be patient.

- *Avoid jumping to conclusions–it's probably not as bad as you think.* Cultural stereotypes abound concerning alternative religious practices; misconceptions, apprehensions, and fears run rampant. Ask for pertinent information, if you're curious or confused.

- *Stay away from lengthy philosophical arguments,* especially when they're going nowhere. Give up trying to change another person's mind.

- *Maintain boundaries if you are in your own home.* If you don't want your daughter-in-law to light the candles for the Jewish Sabbath in your Lutheran home, ask her not to. You can invite her to do it quietly in her bedroom, instead.

- *Keep a sense of humor!* There *is* something endearing about seeing your son trying to balance on one foot like a whooping crane as he practices his Tai Chi in the middle of the living room. Have a chuckle at your own uptightness.

- *Remember–your children's choices are not about you, they're about them.* If you find yourself feeling reactive, repeat to yourself, "It's not personal. It's not personal. It's not personal."

- *If your children, or nieces or nephews, are in an inter-faith relationship, and their children belong to two traditions, find a way to honor both religions without diminishing either.* At a Christmas dinner I attended in one interfaith family, the grandfather said Catholic grace and then asked his Jewish grand-daughter to say the blessing in Hebrew.

- *Realize that your family members want your acknowledgment, not necessarily your agreement.* You don't have to get up at sunrise and pray with them, just let them know you love them and that whatever they're doing is their choice, even if you don't understand it.

- *Time is a great healer.* Once you're sitting around the fireplace together drinking hot chocolate, you'll remember that your "black sheep" son or daughter or other family member is essentially the same person that you've known and loved for years.

- *Make your life a true spiritual life.* Kindness, generosity and compassion are the virtues human beings strive for. To practice them in our daily lives greatly furthers our evolution as a species.

8

Leaving Your Family Problems On Their Doorstep

All right, you've made it through the holidays in one piece and are now safe and cozy in your own bed (or comfortable in your own kitchen), so why are you still bickering with your husband in the *same* way your parents nag one another? Why are you having dreams of your kindergarten teacher and your long-deceased dog, Spot? Why are you worried that your thirty-four-year-old daughter isn't getting enough to eat when she's really old enough to take care of herself?

Returning to the metaphor of the family as an ecosystem as described in Chapter Two, attending the family holiday is like suddenly being returned to your childhood environment, although your whole life since you left, or since your kids moved away, has been spent in an entirely different climate. The atmospheric conditions, sensory-stimulation, language and emotional systems are unlike what you have grown accustomed to in your independent life, but they are also familiar and seductive, bringing you back to old identities, habits and behaviors that you left behind (or thought you did) long ago. The patterns you have tried to work yourself out of will slip back in through the tiniest cracks, regardless of how "conscious" you have become of them.

Think of this "after the holiday" effect as a type of psychological jet lag. Recognize that your physical and psychic systems are processing a long trip on many inner levels, and give yourself some space to ground yourself and integrate the experience. If you are the type of person who wants to make use of the holiday as an opportunity for growth (which you are in no way obliged to do–surviving it is enough!), observe yourself closely at this time without judgment, watching the subtle changes in your behavior and thinking. Consider what was positive and what was negative about the experience, and what you would like to do differently next time.

Sometimes a good holiday is harder to stomach than one that was blatantly negative. An easy visit following a rough childhood or a difficult period of childraising tends to give rise to the false hope that things will suddenly be

different forever, and you may find yourself building cas-
tles on sand. There is nothing *wrong* with a good visit–you
should aspire to it always, but see it for what it is. On the
other hand, a happy visit may be the welcome indication
that you are maturing and learning how to roll with the
punches.

SOME FINAL SUGGESTIONS FOR AN EASY WINDING DOWN:

- *Allow time for re-adjustment.* Even if you make it
  through the visit with flying colors, unexpected emotions may suddenly surface in the safety of your own
  home, or relationship quarrels may appear out of
  nowhere.

- *Don't judge yourself unnecessarily* for any difficult feelings or interactions that occurred during the visit.
  Realize you've just been through a challenging situation.

- *Arrange it so you don't have to go back to work the day
  after the visit.* Tack a few days onto the end of the holiday visit for your own little vacation.

- *If you're feeling insecure about what happened, call
  up someone you can talk to in your family* and have a

conversation about how it went for him or her and how it was for you. Consider how you might wish to do it differently in the future.

- *Spend some relaxed time reconnecting with your friends and/or spouse.* It will help ground you in familiar soil.

- *If you have children, pay extra attention to their adjustment period.* They may need additional affection or acknowledgment from you.

- *If you're completely out of whack upon returning home, get support from some friends, a therapist, or a group.* There is nothing wrong with needing "a little help from your friends."

- *Doing something creative is an excellent way to defuse excess tension.* Drawing, painting, singing, dancing, journal keeping and writing poetry are good places to start. (These are also good ways for your children to integrate the visit.)

- *Exercise is vital.* If you're not in shape, choose something non-vigorous such as walking, gardening, or stretching. If you exercise regularly, continue your routine.

- *Relax!* Whatever is coming to the surface, remember it is really not the end of the world.

9

The Point Of It All

The real point of the holiday–or of any family gathering–is the celebration of life: gathering together in good company, remembering the sacred, being compassionate and offering service.   I'm not talking about mouthing empty words or performing meaningless gestures–celebrating with the people we love doesn't mean showering them with presents or getting drunk in their honor. The sacred is not only found in a picture of Jesus. The sacred is always available even in the most mundane of circumstances, and may or may not be available in so-called holy settings. Compassion is not simply donating your cast-off clothes to the Salvation Army. Service is not only about doing, doing, doing. The point is to be real with yourself and real with others; to stand for what you know to be true and to live in the integrity of that. When you dare to look at any situation with clarity and piercing honesty, you can then more wisely choose to act appropriately.

Many a client comes in before the holidays with this problem or that problem, supposedly not knowing what to do about it, but when I ask them what they'd tell their best friend to do in such a situation, they articulate clearly and precisely what they themselves need to do. We all know what needs to be done–whether it is visiting our parents and bringing some enthusiasm to their otherwise humdrum lives; or honoring our child's request to have a non-alcoholic holiday because he or she is struggling to stay sober; or staying home with our own family and recreating the holidays in a way that will be meaningful to us, although it may not have anything to do with "the family tradition."

In the process of maturing into a more caring and compassionate human being (and this can begin, or deepen, at any age) you go through many stages and cycles. An early stage is complacency: You go along with others' plans for the family gathering because you're afraid of losing their love and approval. You obey as a child would, even if you are seventy-five years old. The next level is rebellion, or boundary-making (sometimes called "*orneriness*" in later

years): You are individuating from your family members–standing on your own as a person for the first time,
or establishing your independence and a new lifestyle as
an older adult—so you may refuse to join, or host, the
family holiday. The third stage is surrender: That looks
much like the first stage, only now you are acquiescing
from a place of knowing who you are–neither needing to
prove yourself by acting against your family members'
wishes, nor going along with their wishes because you
fear disapproval. You surrender to the situation because
they are your parents, or your kids; because you are in
their home, or they really want to come to yours; because
you know your parents aren't going to change if they
haven't in the past sixty-five years, or because you want to
honor the differences that your children possess; and,
most of all, because the true holiday spirit is about giving
of yourself.

> Going home for the holidays used to be a sad
> time for me because I always longed for a more
> authentic connection and closeness with my
> family. There were so many unspoken com-
> munications, and it was hard to accept the fact
> that the visit was not going to come close to the
> way I wanted it to be. Over time, the holidays
> have become something different. I have made
> my peace with my parents and other relatives,

and I am grateful for the opportunity to give of myself in any ways I can to make their lives easier and happier during these times.

The importance of a sense of humor cannot be overstated. Real humor is not making sarcastic and demeaning jokes to break the tension during Thanksgiving dinner. Humor is a wise quality of lightness and perspective that is based upon the recognition that we are all human beings struggling to find our way through our daily lives. It is the ability to laugh at ourselves, recognizing that our beliefs and ideals are probably as strange to others as theirs are to us. Even if the situation is awful, there is humor to be found in it. There is a way to laugh with others even when there are differences among us, and this kind of humor has a way of bringing people into honest communication with one another.

My final wish, hope, desire, aspiration and supplication is that you may have a truly happy holiday, and a nurturing and enlivening family gathering.

A Few Of My Favorites
For Further Reading

Family Psychology

Bradshaw, John. *Bradshaw On The Family.* Pompano Beach, FL: Health Communications, 1988.
Napier, Augustus Y., and Carl A. Whittaker. *The Family Crucible.* New York: Harper and Row, 1978.

Health

Thomas, Lalitha. *Ten Essential Foods.* Prescott, AZ: Hohm Press, 1997.
Ryan, Regina Sara, and John W. Travis, MD. *The Wellness Workbook.* Berkeley, CA: Ten Speed Press, 1988.

Children

Berends, Polly Berrien. *Whole Child-Whole Parent.* New York: Harper & Row, 1983.
Pearce, Joseph Chilton. *Magical Child: Rediscovering Nature's Plan for Our Children.* New York: Dutton, 1992.

Gay and Lesbian

Bernstein, Robert A. *Straight Parents, Gay Children: Keeping Families Together.* New York: Thunder's Mouth Press, 1995.
Marcus, Eric. *Is It A Choice? Answers to 300 of the Most Frequently Asked Questions About Gays and Lesbians.* New York: HarperCollins, 1993.

Spiritual Issues

Moore, Thomas. *Care of the Soul.* New York: HarperCollins, 1994.
Fields, Rick. *Chop Wood, Carry Water.* Los Angeles: J.P. Tarcher, distributed by Houghton Mifflin, 1984.

Crisis and Grief

Bridges, William. *Transitions: Making Sense of Life's Changes.* Reading, MA: Addison-Wesley, 1980.

Stearns, Ann Kaiser. *Living Through Personal Crisis.* New York: Ballantine Books, 1985.